D1429814

Principles of
International Marketing

Principles of Export Guidebooks

Series Editor: Michael Z. Brooke

Principles of
International Marketing

Julia Spencer

First published 1994

Blackwell Publishers
108 Cowley Road
Oxford OX4 1JF
UK

238 Main Street
Cambridge, Massachusetts 02142
USA

British Library Cataloguing in Publication Data
A CIP catalogue record for this book is available from the British Library.

Library of Congress Cataloging-in-Publication Data
A CIP catalog record for this book is available from the Library of Congress.

ISBN 0-631-19251-4

Typeset in 11½pt on 13½pt Garamond Light by Aitch Em Wordservice, Aylesbury, Buckinghamshire, Great Britain.

Printed in Great Britain by Hartnolls Limited, Bodmin, Cornwall.

This book is printed on acid-free paper.

Contents

List of Figures
and Tables

Foreword

This Foreword is written to welcome the fifth of our series of export texts, Principles of International Marketing, by Julia Spencer.

Mrs Spencer is The Institute's Home-Study Tutor for this subject and the book promises to be essential to those seeking Institute qualifications as well as others seeking to improve their export performance.

The Earl of Limerick, President,
The Institute of Export

Series Editor's Introduction

In launching the fifth book in this series of guidebooks to the profession of exporting, the series editor – along with others associated with the project – is pleased to welcome Julia Spencer as its author.

This book on International Marketing picks up on previous titles to provide a practical outline of the key issues. The author's contribution to the development of you, the reader, rests on her long experience and I present this book with great pride to the exporting public.

The main focus of Julia's book is on putting together a strategy for entering an overseas market. Particular attention is paid to selecting the most appropriate sales channel, and this is dealt with in detail.

May I welcome you, the reader, and hope to meet you again as the other books in the series appear on all aspects of export which you need to know – law (for the non-lawyer), transport and distribution, trade and payments, market research, and export management, in addition to the first book in the series which is review of the whole subject.

Michael Z. Brooke

About The Institute of Export Examinations

The Institute is grateful for the initiative of Michael Z. Brooke, the series editor, and Blackwell Publishers in publishing this unique series of books specially written for the Professional Examinations.

The authors for the series have been carefully selected and have specialized knowledge of their subjects, all being established lecturers or examiners for the Professional Examinations.

The books have been written in a style that is of benefit not only to students of The Institute but also to commercial organizations seeking further information about specific aspects of international trade.

Professionalism in export is vital for every company if they are to compete successfully in world markets and this new series of books provides a sound basis of knowledge for all those seeking a professional qualification in export through The Institute of Export's Professional Examinations.

The book covers the following parts of The Institute's syllabus.

International Marketing (Export Distribution)

Objectives of the Syllabus

Export marketing is a term which covers the entire export contract from drawing board to after-sales service. For example, inefficient export practice destroys the value of first-rate promotion in the market-place. This subject, therefore, in addition to the following syllabus, calls for a review of all the areas covered in the Institute of Export Professional Part 1 Examination, that is, Principles of Marketing, Principles of Law relating to Overseas Trade, International Trade and Payments, and International Physical Distribution. This essential revision will be reflected in a question in the examination paper which will be obligatory for all students and candidates will have to obtain 25 marks out of a possible 40 to pass; failure in this question will result in failure in the complete paper.

World markets

1 An outline knowledge of the major economic, social, political and cultural characteristics and trade patterns of the major market groupings in the world economy and their impact on British export performance:

Western Europe
Africa
Middle East
Far East
Eastern Europe
North America
Central and Latin America
Indian sub-continent
Australia
North America

2 The formation and operation of Common Markets and Free Trade Areas, and other arrangements, for example, OPEC and their impact on British exports and imports.

3 An awareness that:

   (a) Common Markets and Free Trade Areas do not necessarily coincide with geographical groupings in 1;

   (b) there are often 'natural' markets which cross political boundaries, for example, Netherlands and Flemish Belgium;

   (c) there may be market segments which are independent of political boundaries and can be treated as world markets, for example, jeans, Coca-Cola.

Distribution

1 Physical distribution
   - the nature of physical distribution and the role within the firm
   - total distribution cost concept
   - physical distribution costs in relation to the firm's cost structure
   - analysis of physical distribution problems and their possible solutions
   - role of channels of distribution in physical distribution.

2 Channels of distribution
   importance of selecting the best possible channel considerations when contemplating changes in channels of distribution

   (a) UK channels of distribution
       domestic manufacturers; pick-a-back; group sales arrangements; export manager arrangements; UK buying offices; export houses; consortia; advantages and disadvantages of each; appointments and agreements

   (b) Overseas channels of distribution
       - direct
       - agents; distributors; exclusive outlets; specialist outlets
       - advantages and disadvantages of each
       - appointments and agreements

(c) Developments and patterns in overseas channels of distribution systems, for example decline of wholesalers
(d) Company owned channels of distribution
  - marketing subsidiary; contract manufacturers; assembly; full manufacture
  - advantages and disadvantages of each
  - control
(e) Licensing/franchising
  - types
  - negotiation process and agreements
(f) Joint ventures
  - types
  - control arrangements
  - negotiation process and agreements
(g) Miscellaneous, for example, mail order; travelling representatives
(h) Other considerations
  - relative advantages of each of the channels of distribution systems (a)-(g)
  - legal implications of agreements
  - arrangements for the chosen channel of distribution and credit, financial, promotional, and so on
  - consignment stocks
  - prompt attention to communications

3 Visiting overseas markets
  - objectives and terms of reference
  - arrangements beforehand and conduct during the visit
  - reporting back
  - use of foreign language
  - promotional activities, for example, exhibitions, literature

4 After-sales service
  - handling complaints
  - guarantees and warranties; legal requirements
  - location and handling of stocks of spares
  - methods of carrying out after-sales service.

R.T. Ebers FIEx,
Director of Education & Training,
The Institute of Export

1

Selecting a Marketing Strategy: Case Study 1

The first three chapters of this book take a detailed look at how international marketing decisions are made in practice, illustrated with case studies taken from The Institute of Export examinations in this subject. The practice of summarizing a situation in a few paragraphs, as in a case study, is always a useful starting point for making business decisions. Because of this they should be of equal benefit to Institute students and the general reader alike. Students taking this examination are required to apply their knowledge not just of marketing, but also of international trade and payments, law and international physical distribution. Readers who are unfamiliar with these subjects are referred to the companion volumes in this series.

The case study question forms the first part (Section A) of the examination paper. It is compulsory, and students need to achieve at least 25 marks out of a total of 40 in this question. Failure in the question means failure in the paper. The prominence given here to Section A is a reflection of the difficulty which students have with this question, and the high failure rate in it. (On the other hand, virtually nobody fails Section B, so take heart!)

The three case studies give worked examples of three very different questions from past examinations, chosen to give readers the widest possible scope for applying their knowledge. The first question is about a company which makes products for the veterinary market; the second question deals with a manufacturer of heavy-duty vehicles for use in developing countries; and the third is about exporting a service (interior design). In each case the reader is asked to submit proposals for developing exports: by selecting a suitable market and the most effective distribution channel within it, by developing a suitable promotional strategy, by recommending the most efficient method of transport, and by justifying it all with a budget, showing how the venture will make a profit. The difficulty is not in making individual decisions, but in making interrelated decisions which make a convincing case, given the circumstances.

It is important to stress that there is no single correct answer to these questions, and that no two acceptable answers will be the same. There is no reason why a totally different solution from that suggested should not be equally acceptable.

By way of illustration, the first worked example is given with two completely different answers. (Subsequent examples will discuss different options, but only one complete answer will be given.)

Readers are advised to read the question several times, and then give thought to how they would answer it, before reading on. It may be useful to take notes; but do not attempt to start answering the question before having a clear idea of everything you want to say. Too many students panic into trying to get all their thoughts down on paper, only to discover that they cannot follow them all through. There is a long process of elimination to go through first; nothing should be written down at this stage, other than rough notes and calculations.

Case Study 1

A UK pharmaceutical company, specializing in veterinary products, has developed a unique method of diagnosing diseases in farm animals. The product has been highly successful in the UK and within two years of launch sales are running at £1,500,000 per year. Manufacturing and selling costs are £8 per unit. The lowest selling price is £10 per unit. The product has been protected by patent, worldwide.

The product

The product comes in a form which can be administered by a farmer or a veterinary surgeon and, when used regularly (approximately every 6-8 weeks), it enables an early diagnosis to be made of the more common diseases in cattle, sheep and pigs. Should a test prove positive, then action can be taken to prevent the disease developing. The cost of treatment of the diseases which the product diagnoses, when they have developed, can be very high, or, in some cases, it can mean that the animal, and perhaps other animals in the herd, have to be slaughtered. The product, when used regularly, can, therefore, save a farmer a considerable amount of money. The product contains sufficient material to test five animals.

Marketing

In the UK, the product is sold direct to large farmers at £15 per unit and to veterinary surgeons who receive a discount of 25 per cent and also to wholesalers who receive a discount of 33 per cent. The company has a small salesforce in the UK of 10 people, based in the main agricultural areas, who sell direct to the farmers or to veterinary surgeons or to wholesalers. The salesforce sell other company products as well. The product is advertised in farmers' and veterinary surgeons' trade magazines and is also exhibited at agricultural shows. As yet, the product has not been sold abroad.

The Task

You have been appointed to develop the overseas business for this product and have been granted a budget of £45,000 for the next twelve months, which is to cover the extra marketing variable and fixed costs involved in developing the chosen overseas markets.

You are to present an initial short report which outlines your recommendations on the actions which the company should take in order to achieve the given objectives. This must include your recommendations covering the following points:

1 Which market, or markets, should be developed, giving reasons for your choice.
2 Outline marketing strategies for the chosen market, or markets.
3 Any problems, and their solution, regarding physical distribution, documentation, payment and so on.
4 A quantified budget.

To Answer

In the face of a number of (usually conflicting) reactions to these questions students often do not know how to start answering them. The answer is simple – before writing anything, read the instructions! In this case they are quite explicit; the task is:

1 to develop overseas business for the product;
2 to do so within a budget of £45,000;
3 to recommend markets, with reasons;
4 to recommend marketing strategies;
5 to identify any problems regarding transport, documentation, payment and other costs; and
6 to submit a budget for the proposals.

We are not told, but can reasonably assume, that we should also make a profit in the process.

Note the limiting factor of £45,000; every case study has a financial objective which must be achieved. It is particularly important to identify this, since it will limit the choices open to us. The first step therefore is to define the task, numerically wherever possible, since all our proposals will be geared to achieving it.

Having stated clearly what our objective is, we now need to look at the factors we must take into account to achieve this – to conduct a situation (or 'SWOT') analysis. This helps the process of elimination and gives pointers for action – there are often clues in the information. For instance:

1   The company has a very limited export budget of £45,000; this rules out options like setting up a manufacturing plant overseas, which would cost far more than this. It also limits the number of markets which can be entered.

2   The product is profitable and not price-sensitive; it sells for a markup of up to 87.5 per cent of the manufacturing and selling costs.

3   There are many distribution channels available: already the product is marketed direct to farmers through wholesalers and vets; agricultural cooperatives are at least one more possibility.

4   The company has no knowledge of export procedures. How will it handle such day-to-day problems as documentation and payment?

5   We are talking about a unique, successful, repeat-purchase product, easy to use and offering considerable cost-saving, and protected by worldwide patents.

6   There is no known competition, but it is necessary to establish the product quickly before the competition catches up.

7   No information is available about local legislation (such as product certification) which will affect the company's ability to enter a market.

8   The company sells other products; its resources may not be adequate to exploit the potential of this one. (The small budget suggests that this is the case.)

9   Is product liability insurance needed? This is a major cost in some markets.

10 Are EC farm subsidies an opportunity to exploit? (NB: This paper was set in 1991.)

We may feel that there is not enough information to complete the SWOT analysis. For example:

1   What is the market potential? We know nothing about the numbers of cattle, sheep and pigs in likely markets, or location or sizes of farms (and nor can we be expected to). How then can we make sales forecasts, or establish whether a market is large enough to enter?

2   There is little information on which to base sales forecasts.

3 Even if we know the market size, how can we tell whether production capacity is adequate to satisfy it? There is no point in getting large orders if the company cannot fulfil them.

4 Has the product been developed to international standards, or is adaptation or local certification (the latter is a lengthy process) needed before it can go on sale overseas?

5 We have no way of knowing what the proposed export operation will cost – the product has not been sold abroad before and the company has little export knowledge.

6 Are the diseases connected with climate? If so, this will limit the countries for which the product is suitable.

So, there are gaps in the information; what are we to do about them? There are several ways round this! We can say what we would do in real life; or we can make assumptions, giving reasons for what we say. It is important not to run away from the problem by failing to mention it. However, beware of saying that further market research is needed; examiners see it as an escape route. If we take the problems in turn, we can see how they might be dealt with – readers will no doubt have their own solutions.

Profile of the farming markets

We can make our proposals about known agricultural countries, but subject to confirmation by desk research; or we can estimate the sales volume needed to reach the target, and make the proposals conditional on the market being large enough to achieve this. Alternatively, we can assume that research has already been undertaken, and that the proposals are a result of this.

Sales forecasts

Because of the product's rapid success in the United Kingdom, it should also be successful elsewhere. If second year sales in the United Kingdom are £1,500,000, first year sales were probably around £500,000. First year export sales of 10 per cent of United Kingdom turnover (£150,000) should be easily achievable. (This is a conservative estimate, and can probably be easily exceeded; but it is wise to err on the cautious side. If sales are higher, so much the better.)

Production capacity

Since we are told simply to 'develop the overseas business' (a vague brief), we can assume the company can handle any sales which result. Or, we can qualify our proposals by saying that the production manager has confirmed there is no problem. A more imaginative way round this is to license a foreign manufacturer to produce the goods – a profitable option, in view of the product's potential and the company's limited resources.

Product licensing

Because the product has been patented worldwide, it is reasonable to assume that it will be acceptable worldwide as well. Alternatively, we can assume that since it was produced in the United Kingdom, it is to European Community standards; or, since export markets are being considered, that it is capable of being modified for local standards; or that desk research has revealed that no licensing is necessary. (Since the test can be administered by a farmer, it seems that no specialist veterinary knowledge is necessary).

For costs, we have to guess, use common sense, and draw on our own experience. Few, if any, readers will have launched a veterinary product overseas and be able to say what a product launch costs, for example. In real life we would probably work out what we could afford, decide what we wanted to do, and then ask an advertising agency how best to achieve it within the budget. That is what we can do here.

Regarding climate, there is a choice. Either we can decide on a market such as France or Holland, which both have similar conditions to the United Kingdom, since the same diseases are likely to occur there; or we can go for very different countries –

Argentina, Brazil, South Africa or India – on the assumption that animals suffer the same diseases wherever they are, regardless of climate.

The assumptions we make are now starting to influence our decisions; some options are being opened to us, while other possibilities are being eliminated. (It is important to stress again that any one of a number of answers could be correct.) Any case or assumption based on the facts available will be accepted, provided sensible reasons are given.)

At this stage it is possible to start making decisions. The principal one is which market(s) to enter. This is not necessarily the first thing to decide, but it is as good a starting point as any. What are the criteria for our target market? (The characteristics of different markets are discussed in more detail in chapter 4.)

We should be looking for an agricultural country with large enough numbers of sheep, pigs and cattle to justify entering it, sufficient money to pay for the goods, and adequate distribution channels to handle them. In view of the company's limited resources and its need to stay ahead of competitors, the market should be one which can be entered as easily as possible. Some of the areas which can be considered are:

1 The European Community. A large market which has the advantages (for the new exporter) of being close to hand and easy to service, with minimal transport, documentation and payment problems, and strong agricultural communities in most countries; affluent markets, but where agriculture is characterised by overproduction and the failure of the Common Agricultural Policy (CAP).
2 The United States. Differing state and federal legislation make export difficult, as does the size of the country, but the country is English-speaking, so there is no language problem.
3 South America. Brazil and Argentina, for example, are developing countries with large cattle-rearing areas and manufacturing ability; import restrictions make direct export impossible, but licensing local production would be a good option, in view of the company's limited resources.
4 New Zealand. An English-speaking country with pro-British attitudes and strong agriculture, but transport will be expensive

because of distance; current economic problems could make export difficult.

5 Eastern Europe. Farming based economies, in need of western knowhow and technology, but with little money to pay for them; undeveloped distribution channels because of the confusion since the collapse of state control.

6 South Africa. A country with the ability to manufacture the product and market it to neighbouring territories; strong agriculture, good transport, but with economic problems and political uncertainty.

So there are plenty of options open. We do not need to decide on the market at this stage – it is sensible to look at the question in more detail first.

Many exam questions require the student to select a sectoral market as well as the geographical one – for example, to decide whether to attack the industrial or consumer market first, or to target one industry rather than another. In this case we are aiming only at one sector – agriculture – so the choice does not arise.

Some questions require the student to choose to export one product out of several, giving reasons for the decision. In this case there is no need, since there is only one product. Be prepared for this in future questions, though.

Once we have gone some way towards identifying a market and a product, we need to identify the **distribution channels** which will get the product to consumers most effectively. (The characteristics of different distribution channels are discussed in more detail later in the book.) Here the end user is the farmer; in the home market the company sells direct, but we cannot afford to take on sales staff to do this overseas. Nor can we assume that the channels used in the home market will be available overseas – vets may be limited by their professional body from selling, for example. So, we have to look at other options: licensing (particularly suitable for the more distant markets); mail order (good for reaching remote areas, and widely used in countries like Germany, even to sell industrial products); or a distributor – most likely an agricultural cooperative or wholesaler - who will buy in bulk and sell the product on. The decision will depend on the market.

We also need to decide what form of promotion is most appropriate, given the product, distribution channel, and target market. (Promotion is covered in more detail in chapter 13.) This will depend on the distribution channel chosen. If we go for the licensing option, then the licensee will take responsibility for both manufacturing and marketing the product. Similarly, a distributor will handle promotion locally, though the exporting company might well be expected to contribute to a product launch. What is clear is that the message must reach farmers, and that it will have more impact if it comes through vets; common sense tells us this, and it is backed up by the experience in the home market. If vets are unable or unwilling to be involved in promotion, then it must be done through wholesalers, or done directly to the farmers. It is likely to include:

1 Point-of-sale displays – samples, demonstrations, posters and so on.
2 Good publicity in the trade press (aimed both at the farmers and vets), in addition to the national press, quoting success stories and the results of clinical trials.
3 A product launch at a suitable agricultural fair.
4 Suitable sales literature in the language(s) of the market, as well as repackaging, with clear instructions suitable for local requirements.

Readers may well have other suggestions. (Note that no advertising has been suggested; promotion is frequently equated with advertising, but there are many other, more cost-effective, ways to reach the end user.)

Do we need to make any decisions about pricing? (We need an estimate of sales in order to work out the profitability of the venture.) For direct export, it seems that pricing will not be critical, since the product commands a high price and can be shown to pay for itself. In the home market, manufacturing and selling costs total £8 per unit; for the European Community, we can comfortably assume costs of £10 per unit to cover the extra costs of freight, insurance, documentation, and so on; for further afield, £12. For budget purposes assume a discounted selling price of £15 (for direct sales it could be as high as £20).

If selling under licence, the company will receive a royalty of around five per cent of sales, plus signing fee and sometimes payments for technical support. The selling price will have to be lower in less affluent developing countries (though production costs will be lower as well). There is no information provided to help us with this, so we have to guess – say £7 per unit in Brazil and Argentina, £10 in South Africa and New Zealand, and £12 in the United States. This means income respectively of 35p, 50p and 60p per unit sold.

What about **documentation, insurance,** and **payment?** With direct export, the company's responsibilities will be defined by the appropriate Incoterm. If the product is sold on a Delivered Duty Paid (DDP) basis, then the company will deal with all formalities up to the point of delivery: packing, marking, customs clearance, documentation, insurance, and transport. In the case of local licensing, no physical movement of goods is involved, but the principal concern will be the drafting of a contract, acceptable to both parties, and satisfactory under the law of both countries. In both cases terms of payment will also have to be established.

What will it all cost? If exporting direct, most of the budget will be spent on promotion, with a comparatively small allocation for travel (if within the EC) and research. In the case of licensing, it will be important to have a properly drawn up legal agreement, acceptable to both parties and checked by legal advisers in both countries; this will constitute the highest cost, followed by training and travel (since more distant markets will be involved). The licensing company is not normally expected to undertake promotion, but may decide to support its licensees by global promotion to establish the brand.

The picture is becoming clearer. Now we have to start to make a financial justification for what we want to do; this starts with a sales forecast. For direct sales, we can now see that the conservative estimate of the assumed sales of £150,000 (10,000 units @ £15) can contain both the cost of sales (10,000 units @ £10, as assumed above), and additional marketing costs of £45,000. Sales can be expected to expand rapidly in the second year. The following forecast allows for further market development in the second year.

	Year 1 £000	Year 2 £000
sales	150	450
cost of sales (£10/unit)	(100)	(300)
extra marketing costs	(45)	(25)
net profit	5	125

The above figures assume that overheads are covered by the United Kingdom operation, since no information is given about them.

For a licensing operation there are no production costs to recoup; these are borne by the licensee. Instead it is necessary to work out the break-even point, that is, the number of units which must be sold in order to cover the £45,000 marketing costs. If the average revenue to the company is around 50 pence per unit, then we need sales of around 90,000 units to justify the venture. This is unlikely to be achieved in the first year, since it will be several months at least before the licensees start to produce the goods locally. However, we are not told that the extra £45,000 marketing costs have to be recouped in the first year. After the initial outlay there will be little, if any, further cost to the company during the licence period, whereas royalties can be expected to increase dramatically. In the circumstances, we can make a good case for investing £45,000 in anticipation of long-term benefits.

We can now start to finalize decisions and write the report; up to now any writing should have been confined to rough notes and calculations. It may be necessary to juggle figures at this stage to balance them, and to exclude some of the options which have been considered. The important thing is to make a reasoned case, with consistent decisions. It is clear that equally good cases can be made for direct export to neighbouring countries, and licensing the product in more distant ones. This does not mean that other options will be wrong; any sensible, consistent proposals will be acceptable to the examiner. The following outlines the case for each – students may like to try writing an answer themselves before reading on. Note that the answer should be in report form, and the order of the questions – 1, 2 and so on – should be adhered to in the report.

Direct Export Option

Report to: Managing Director

From: Export Manager

Subject: Development of overseas business for new diagnostic veterinary product

Introduction

The following preliminary proposals are subject to desk research to quantify the size of the proposed market, and to confirm the existence of suitable distribution channels. They also assume that production capacity can handle the increased business.

1 Which market(s) should be developed

I recommend that in the first year of export we develop business in France and Holland, for the following reasons:

1 Both countries are heavily dependent on agriculture.
2 Both countries being members of the European Community, there are minimal formalities and payment problems.
3 They have similar climates to the United Kingdom, so livestock will suffer from the same diseases as exist here.
4 Minimal communication problems; English is widely spoken in Holland, and French is the most common second language in the United Kingdom.
5 Both countries are developed, stable economies with good distribution networks.
6 There is plenty of published information to assist research and help define the market.

7 Both are affluent markets which can afford a quality product.
8 They are easily accessible in case of problems.

The company should also consider longer-term plans in order to establish the product in other markets ahead of the competition, but this is outside the scope of the present report.

2 Outline marketing strategies

Product: No choice.

Place: The prime concern is to identify suitable distribution channels, since this will affect remaining marketing decisions. The best option, if available, will be to appoint local distributors already supplying to farmers and veterinary surgeons. This will probably be a veterinary or pharmaceutical wholesaler, possibly an agricultural cooperative. Having a distributor will give us the advantages of immediate contact with the market, and having a single outlet to deal with. The distributor will not be required to hold large stocks, since both markets can be readily supplied from the United Kingdom.

Price: The product is not price-sensitive. If export costs (manufacturing, transport, documentation, packing, insurance and product/public liability insurance) total £10, we can assume a discounted selling price of £15 to the distributor which still allows for some flexibility.

Promotion: This is primarily the distributor's responsibility, but the company should assist with launch costs. This will include:

1 Exhibiting at an agricultural fair.
2 Publicity, especially in veterinary and farming journals and to farmers' unions.
3 Repackaging, with instructions in French or Dutch.
4 Point of sale materials, demonstrating the product's effectiveness and ease of use.

Preliminary costings for this have been given by our advertising agency (see below).

3 Physical distribution

The goods will be transported by road, since this is quick, cheap, and flexible. Transport will be in full container loads (FCL) for security and in order to minimise transport costs. Documentation required within the European Community is minimal:

1 A commercial invoice showing community status.
2 Packing list, if more than one containerload is sent on a single invoice.
3 Insurance certificate.
4 CMR note (the road transport document).

It is assumed that there is nothing dangerous about the product and that no special packing is needed. Deliveries can be on a door-to-door, inclusive basis (DDP – Incoterms 1990) on open account with 60 days' credit, subject to satisfactory credit references and first payment in advance. It may be convenient to invoice the distributor in local currency.

Since the company has little export experience, it should decide whether to use a freight forwarder (for transport, documentation, insurance and packing), or to set up a shipping department in house. The latter is recommended in view of the product's long-term export potential, and staff should be sent on an Institute of Export course to be trained in documentation and any other aspects of export.

4 Budget

The following figures assume sales in France and Holland of £150,000 each in the first year of export – this is a conservative figure which is likely to be exceeded:

sales	300,000 (20,000 units)
cost of sales (£10/unit)	(200,000)
extra marketing costs	(45,000)
net profit	55,000 (18%)

The marketing budget is to be spent as follows:

trade fairs (2)	20,000
publicity	5,000
travel	1,000
research	8,000
translation and packaging	5,000
posters, sales literature etc.	5,000
staff training	1 000
total	45,000

Licensing Option

Introduction

I have been asked to submit recommendations for developing the overseas business of the new veterinary diagnostic product.
    In view of:

1 the company's limited resources (budget, export experience);
2 the enormous potential for the product, indicated by rapid growth in the home market; and
3 the importance of capitalizing on the technical advantage as fast as possible.

I recommend licensing local manufacturers to produce and market the product in selected markets. Licensing is a quick, low-cost way of securing market entry with minimum risk and involvement to the licensing company.

1 Which market(s) should be developed

Assuming the treatment is suitable for different climatic and environmental conditions, I recommend local licensing in:

1 the agricultural states of the United States, South America (Brazil, for export to other Latin American Integration Association (ALADI) countries);
2 Southern Africa; and
3 Australia and New Zealand.

Licensing is particularly appropriate for these more distant markets because local import restrictions and the cost of transport make direct export difficult.

It is assumed that no field trials or lengthy product licensing procedures are necessary to enter the markets.

2 Marketing strategy

The first task is to research suitable locations for the proposed venture, having regard to:

1 manufacturing facilities and expertise;
2 access to transport and markets
3 the structure of the pharmaceutical, veterinary and farming markets; and
4 local legislation (national and state) affecting sales of products, in case any modification is needed.

At the same time a search will start for prospective licencees, fulfilling our requirements on:

1 financial stability;
2 technical competence;
3 integrity;
4 marketing and manufacturing capacity; and
5 ability to cover the market.

Approaches will be made through Chambers of Commerce, the Overseas Trade services of the Department of Trade and Industry, banks, trade associations, directories and other sources as well as through informal contacts. The company solicitors will draft a licensing agreement as a basis for discussion and we will put together a file of information on the product and company for prospective licensees. The next step is to short-list candidates, and go to the market to assess their suitability and discuss the terms of the contract. Once agreement has been reached, a contract will be signed, though it will be some time before local production starts because of the time needed to train staff and set up a production line.

Under such an arrangement the licensee takes responsibility for both producing and marketing the product, so our involvement thereafter will be minimal. However, the company should support its licensees worldwide by global branding, for example by sponsoring a major conference on veterinary care.

The company should also be aware that, by selling its know-how to foreign manufacturers, it runs the risk of competition from them once the licence period has expired. Profits from the venture should therefore be used to develop more technical advantages which can be exploited once the agreements run out.

3 Documentation

Because licensing does not involve any physical movement of goods between countries, no transport or other documents are required. It is however extremely important to check local legislation affecting the product, and ensure any formalities are complied with, including legislation on exchange control and remittance of funds. The importance of a detailed legal agreement cannot be underestimated, and it is essential to have the contract vetted by lawyers in the licensee's country since local laws may apply even if the agreement is under English law. The contract must specify how and when royalty payments are to be made. The licensees' selection procedure must include a check on creditworthiness, though credit insurance should also be taken out. The contract must also state clearly which party has responsibility for public and product liability insurance, since adequate cover is essential (particularly in the United States).

4 Budget

Low sales are assumed in Year 1 because of the time taken to put licence arrangements into operation. The following figures are based on an average royalty per unit of 50p, based on 5 per cent of an average selling price of £10. (A lower selling price can be assumed for the developing countries, since production costs will also be lower.)

The figures reflect royalty income only – they do not allow for signing, training, or other fees – and assume sales in four separate markets. Figures are given in sterling, but US and Latin America will be invoiced in dollars.

		Year 1	**Year 2**
total sales (units)		30,000	80,000
total royalty income (£)		15,000	40,000
less marketing costs:			
travel (4 visits @ 1000)	4,000		
legal fees x 4	20,000		
training licensees x 4	4,000		
research	5,000		
publicity	10,000		
miscellaneous	2,000		
		(45,000)	
net profit/loss (cumulative)		(30,000)	10,000

The forecast shows a return of 22 per cent on the £45,000 investment over two years. Sales and profits should increase substantially in year 3, with minimal extra outlay for the company. Overseas licensing is therefore a very attractive prospect and one which should be developed as a matter of priority.
Julia Spencer,
Export Manager.

Note

Although we are only asked for first year proposals, there is no harm in mentioning longer-term plans; it shows we can think strategically. (Good long-term prospects strengthen our case.) Licensing proposals are less specific – we have less information about the markets, but can assume enough to make an acceptable case.

We have seen two possible solutions to the problem and you will probably think of others. A joint European venture with a drug company is one solution which has been suggested; another would be a joint venture in the large developing market of China.

Summary

We have seen how in order to determine a successful marketing strategy we need to:

1 define the task;
2 analyse the situation (look for the clues!);
3 identify the gaps in the information available, and decide what to do about them;
4 select market(s) – both by country and sector;
5 select the product(s), if applicable;
6 decide on the distribution channel;
7 plan promotion;
8 decide on pricing;
9 check requirements for documentation, payment, insurance, and so on;
10 establish what the venture will cost;
11 estimate sales;
12 finalize decisions; and
13 write the report.

You may go through some of these steps in a different order, but if you omit any of them you are likely to overlook a major decision, and you would fail the question in an Institute of Export examination as a result.

2

Selecting a Marketing Strategy: Case Study 2

Now, an example of a much more ambitious question; one in which we have the whole world to choose from. The possibilities here are too numerous to list; the proposals represent one option only. Readers are advised to work through the question themselves before reading further.

The Question

Planos Limited is a company based in the South of England, formed five years ago by an industrial designer and an engineer to manufacture and market a range of rough terrain vehicles. It has been very successful and its most successful and profitable vehicle is a jeep-like 4-wheel-drive vehicle, of very rugged and simple construction, which has been sold all over the world through a network of distributors to civilian customers and commission agents to military customers. Turnover is now in the region of £8 million, of which roughly 80 per cent is exported. Gross profitability is 30 per cent; 40 per cent of sales are in developed countries and 60 per cent in developing countries.

The new product

Planos has just developed a forklift truck, based on the same principles as its jeep, that is, of a rugged and simple construction with 4-wheel-drive and powered by a diesel engine. It has also been designed in such a way that it can be supplied, almost in kit form, that is, the mast, wheels and engine can be fitted locally. It has been tested and found to be very stable. Some of the parts are imported, in particular special tyres from Sweden. Profitability is about the same as for the Jeep.

Expected users

The new forklift truck has been designed with the following users in mind: forestry (where the stability on hillsides is useful); woodyards; brickworks, and steelworks; that is, those applications where operating conditions are bad and where mobile machinery is expected to survive rough treatment.

Competition

The major competition will come from well established companies, such as Volvo, which sell similar rough terrain vehicles and forklift trucks. The new product has, however, certain advantages, in that its price of £20,000 FOB is about 12$^1/_2$ per cent cheaper than similar products and its simple but rugged construction means that it can stand a lot more punishment than the competition.

The Task

You have been appointed Export Manager for this new Planos forklift truck, with the overall objective of ensuring that the investment in it (£500,000) is paid back within three years. You have been asked, initially, to present a report covering the first 12 months, outlining your ideas on how you will develop its exports, including in your report:

1 To which market or markets you will sell, giving adequate reasons for choosing the market or markets.
2 What broad marketing strategy you will recommend.
3 How you will distribute and promote the forklift truck.
4 Any documentation, insurance, transport, financing payment and importing problems which you may meet.
5 A clear budget to quantify your recommendations.

To Answer

Define the task

To develop export sales of the forklift truck, and pay back the investment in it (£500,000) within three years.

To write a report for the first 12 months – though with a budget for three years.

Analyse the situation (look for the clues)

1 Planos is a well-known company, well-established, with a good export operation.
2 There is massive potential for this truck: it is a quality product – competing favourably with Volvo – developed for export markets, suitable for both developed and developing countries and a wide range of applications; it could go anywhere.
3 Big money is involved, and the company is taking a long-term view.

There are no constraints on decisions, provided they meet the target; there is scope for a really ambitious solution.

There are existing export distribution channels (distributors and commission agents): can they be used? (We do not know whether they are reaching the right markets, or are technically competent to handle the truck, give after-sales service, and so on.) Some intermediaries are contractually entitled to handle all their principal's products, though that does not appear to be the case here. Note that employing an intermediary becomes expensive after a certain level of sales; it may be more cost-effective for the company to set up its own operation.

The company also produces jeeps – which have been very successful – and other vehicles, though we know nothing about the latter.

There is a strong indication that we should be looking at developing countries, which account for 60 per cent of sales and for which the simple but rugged truck will be particularly appropriate. But there are high costs in shipping to more distant countries – plus tariff barriers, import restrictions and so on.

There is also a strong clue for some form of local assembly; the truck can be supplied in kit form, and some of its components are imported anyway. This may be an opportunity to take advantage of foreign governments' incentives to encourage invest-ment in the country.

The financial target is an ambitious one, so a lot of attention to figures is needed. The brief is to pay back the initial investment of £500,000. Note that we are not told that this is the cost of the export operation. The wording of the question suggests that the £500,000 is the development costs of the truck – in other words, the cost of the export operation will have to be added in and recovered as well. (Where instructions do not seem very clear, it is acceptable to state what you understand, and write your answer in the light of that.) This is what will be assumed here.

Identify any gaps in the information and decide what to do about them

Financial information is sketchy: the truck's FOB price is £20,000; the company's annual turnover (after five years) is £8 million; 80 per cent of turnover is exported; and gross profit is 30 per cent.

From this, with no information on market demand, we have to try and guess turnover and profitability for the next three years. We can only make sweeping guesses about both.

For profit, we know that gross profit is 30 per cent; this has to be broken down into operating costs and net profit (15 per cent each?). (This will not necessarily be the same overseas). We have assumed above that sales have to cover both the initial investment in the truck and the cost of the export venture. How are we to guess the cost of the export operation in order to submit a budget? (The question suggests that an ambitious solution is called for – one which most readers will not have implemented in real life.) One way round this is to decide what is affordable, and make the proposals conditional on that figure being adequate to finance the new operation.

To make sales forecasts, we can base figures on the success of the company's other products (£8 million turnover in five years). For the new truck, cumulative sales of £5 million over three years look reasonable enough, perhaps achieved as follows:

	Year 1	Year 2	Year 3
sales (£million)	0.75	1.75	2.50
cumulative	0.75	2.50	5.00

This represents sales of 250 trucks – at the FOB price of £20,000 – which sounds much more manageable.

In practice such a sales forecast would have to be backed up with statistics on market demand and size – unfortunately, we do not have that information. Again, all we can do is make the proposals conditional. The company's success so far indicates that the above figures can reasonably be achieved.

So much for the figures. We also lack factual information about likely markets: nature, size and location of industries; import restrictions (common in developing countries); limits to foreign investment; and other factors which will affect Planos' decisions.

The best thing to do is say we shall check the information before proceeding. It is important not to duck issues like this – show you know the problems which must be faced.

Select market(s)

Here, unlike the last case study, we have two decisions to make.

Firstly, there is the choice of territory – and there is a wide range of possibilities:

1   Scandinavia – mountainous terrain in Norway and Sweden, forestry in Sweden and Finland, plus many other industries. The question calls for a bold and confident move. Why not attack Volvo on its home ground? Planos has the advantage. Already some of the components are manufactured in Sweden. We could set up a local assembly operation in order to cut shipping costs. On the other hand, plant and labour costs are high in Sweden. (A more ambitious – but riskier – option is to set up an assembly operation in one of the newly-independent Baltic states, to supply both Scandinavia and the former Soviet Union.)
2   South East Asia – for forestry use in Indonesia and Thailand, rubber plantations in Malaysia, and a host of industries in this rapidly-developing region.
3   Brazil – a huge developing country, with manufacturing capacity, forests, a wide range of industries including steel, and the ability to export to other Latin American countries.
4   China – the market of the future, though it is doubtful if the investment can be repaid within three years.

Secondly, with such a wide range of industries to choose from, we may have to narrow down the choice of sector and launch the jeep to different industries in turn. Even with the large budget, we are unlikely to be able to target all the sectors simultaneously:

1   military
2   forestry
3   woodyards
4   brickworks
5   steelworks

and no doubt others.

Select the product(s)

On the face of it, there is no choice, although the concept of the 'total product' should not be overlooked. Servicing, warranties, customer training, availability of spare parts – all these give the product an edge over the competition, but are difficult to provide in unsophisticated markets.

Decide on the distribution channel

Again there is a wealth of choice, assuming that new arrangements will not conflict with existing ones.

Agents have up to now been used only for the military sector (this truck appears to be for civilian use) but the arrangement is clearly successful. However, because they are paid by commission, agents become expensive after a certain level of sales.

Distributors are also expensive above a certain turnover, although they could also take responsibility for maintenance contracts, service, supply of spares and so on.

There is a strong case for local assembly, particularly in developing markets where there are usually import restrictions. This would have a number of advantages: overheads and labour are cheaper than in the home market; the trucks would be seen as a local product and would therefore be more acceptable, particularly for government purchasing; and there might even be government incentives to encourage foreign investment in the country.

Often the only way of entering a market (for example Nigeria, Brazil) is to establish a joint venture with a local partner. This has the advantage of giving local market knowledge, but there can be conflicts between the partners on such issues as repatriation of profits. Finding a partner with the right match of attributes and experience is a difficult and sometimes lengthy business.

Choice of distribution channel will depend on the market chosen. However, for the sales volume we foresee – several million pounds' worth – employing an agent or distributor will be uneconomic. It will be better for Planos to handle sales itself, and so keep a larger share of the profits.

Plan promotion

This will depend on the market and distribution channel. If distributors are used they will be responsible for promotion, and Planos will not be involved. If the company decides to set up an overseas operation, promotion will be handled by staff there, using a local advertising agency if necessary. In this case promotion might consist of:

1 A launch at a trade fair targeting suitable industries.
2 Publicity, including site visits, to demonstrate the truck's effectiveness.
3 Sales aids – good quality literature (or videos, if feasible) in the local language(s) showing the truck in operation in local conditions.
4 Good public relations aimed at the industry concerned, and direct selling by local sales staff.

Decide on pricing

It does not seem that this truck is price-sensitive, since it is a quality product and represents good value for money. Local assembly may make it possible to sell it at less than the United Kingdom price; but care must be taken not to undervalue it. Pricing decisions are best left to the local manager, if an overseas operation is used. (If selling through distributors, we can base the selling price on the FOB cost, adding a suitable percentage to arrive at the CIF or DDP price, if selling on these terms.)

Establish what the venture will cost

With a question as open as this it is impossible to provide detailed costings. Most readers (like your author) have no idea of the cost of a product launch in Sweden or a salesman in Thailand. No matter – we are not expected to. The important thing is to show how to balance the budget, and to provide for all the costs that arise. In this case we can simply make our proposals subject to being achievable within budget.

We have guessed that operating and manufacturing costs total 85 per cent in the home market. It we assume they are 10 per cent less overseas because of lower wage and other costs, we arrive at the following:

	£000
cumulative sales	5,000
less costs (75%)	(3,750)
investment costs	(500)
balance	750

So, on this forecast we have £750,000 to cover the costs of the export operation and profit (if any; we may only break even). The proposals below assume expenditure of £500,000 on the overseas operation, leaving a modest £250,000 (5 per cent) profit after three years, in the expectation of greater profits once the initial costs have been recovered. Like most of the figures here it is a wild guess, but the important thing is to balance the budget.

Estimate sales

This has already been done, to estimate the funds available for the export venture.

Finalize decisions

Note that this analysis has departed from the sequence laid out above. Instead of costing the operation and then working out what sales are needed to justify it, we have worked back from a sales forecast in order to work out what the company can afford. (The sales forecast is easier to arrive at than the costs, with the little information given.) Also, no reference has been made to documentation requirements. Since the choice of market and distribution channel is so wide, it makes sense to leave the documentation requirements until the market has been decided on. There is no need to follow the steps in the suggested order – provided no important decisions are overlooked. If, as seems likely, we are setting up our own assembly operation in the overseas market, we can now think in terms of . . .

Requirements for documentation, insurance and so on

Readers are referred here to the companion volume in this series, *Principles of International Physical Distribution*, which covers shipping and documentation in detail.

In dealing with a wholly-owned subsidiary, Planos will not need the security usually associated with new customers and more distant markets, such as letters of credit. Transport of the components will be cheapest by sea freight, given the weight of the goods and the distance involved. Parts must be adequately packed to minimize damage or pilferage in transit. A suitable Incoterm should be chosen to specify the responsibilities of the parent and subsidiary companies. (The proposals below assume selling on CIP terms, but local legislation may oblige the subsidiary to buy FOB in order to pay for carriage locally and conserve foreign currency.) The insurance cover required will be dictated by the Incoterm.

We can now begin to write the report.

Proposals for Planos' Export Development

Introduction

Preliminary sales forecasts (see below) suggest a turnover large enough to recoup the development costs within the period indicated, plus market entry costs of up to £500,000. As will be demonstrated, there is a strong case for setting up an overseas subsidiary to assemble the trucks in the market. The following proposals assume that this can be achieved within the above figure. They also assume that there are no local laws which prevent foreign companies from setting up subsidiaries. More detailed proposals and costings will be submitted after my forthcoming visit to the region, as outlined below.

1 Market(s) to be developed

In the first year of operation I recommend setting up an assembly operation in Malaysia, to serve the whole ASEAN area. There are a number of good reasons for choosing this area:

1 Good communications and infrastructure.
2 Political stability and good cooperation within the region.
3 Developing economies with growth potential.
4 Existence of a wide range of industries for which the vehicle can be used.
5 Rough terrain – Thailand, Indonesia – for which the truck is particularly suitable.
6 Widespread use of English, either as an official language or that of business.
7 A presence in the market will deter pirate copies of the truck (always a danger in Asia).

2 Marketing strategy

This cannot be planned in detail until first-hand information is available. The first step will be to identify a suitable location for the proposed venture, having regard to availability of staff, access to ports and local industries, communications, and so forth. At an early stage a local manager, fluent in Malay and English, must be appointed to:

1 Oversee the venture.

2 Set up a local sales operation.
3 Identify market opportunities, submit proposals for promotion, and set priorities, if necessary. (The truck may have to be launched to different sectors in turn.)
4 Coordinate other functions, for example production, to ensure the trucks are available on time.

Consideration should be given to offering a 'total product' including service facilities, availability of spare parts, maintenance training, and a comprehensive product manual, all of which will add value to the truck and establish it as a quality product.

3 How to distribute and promote the truck

There are a number of reasons why Planos should set up an assembly operation:

1 Cheaper labour costs will make the trucks more competitive than imported models.
2 Shipping the components (rather than finished trucks) will cut freight costs and import duties.
3 The trucks are particularly suitable for shipment in kit form.
4 The trucks will be identified as a local product, which will give them an advantage in public contracts.
5 There are often government incentives to encourage such operations, since they provide employment and stimulate the economy.
5 Local operation represents the most cost effective way of realizing the potential of this promising market.

Ideally the assembly should be carried out by a wholly-owned subsidiary, so the company retains maximum profit. If wholly-owned subsidiaries are not permitted under Malaysian legislation, a joint venture with a local partner should be considered. (The proposals assume the former will be possible.) It is hoped that in the longer term the company would develop into full manufacture, and also export to other Asian territories.

As explained above, detailed proposals for promotion will be submitted by the local manager, who will coordinate all activities. These will include recruitment and training of sales staff, product launch, exhibition attendance, and sales aids, as well as the establishment of the extras needed to give the truck added value (service facilities, and so on). An advertising agency with branches all over ASEAN should be retained to assist with these activities.

4 Documentation, insurance, transport and finance

Parts should be shipped in full container loads (FCL) on a CIP basis (Incoterms 1990) to our Malaysian subsidiary. The CIP contract allows for transport by any method and to any port or containerbase. Under these terms we are responsible for:

1 Procuring export licences (if the truck is sold for military purposes).
2 Carrying out customs clearance.
3 Arranging carriage and insurance for contract price plus 10 per cent against buyer's risk, since the risk of loss or damage will pass to the subsidiary company once the container has been delivered to the carrier. (Minimal cover only, that is Institute Cargo Clause C, is required.)
4 Delivering the containerload to the carrier at the containerbase.
5 Obtaining transport and other documents to send to the Malaysian company. An ocean waybill (permitted under CIP terms) is adequate security for an in-house transaction and enables the buyer to take delivery of the goods with minimal formalities.
6 Packing and marking the goods, employing a specialist packer if necessary.

Our colleagues in Malaysia will:

1 Take delivery of the goods locally
2 Clear the goods through customs.

3 Obtain import licences if necessary.
4 Pay duty.

In dealing with a subsidiary company, payment can be made on open account by bank transfer. Since there is no need to send documents through the bank, they can be sent directly to the company in order to speed delivery.

Local regulations may oblige us to sell FOB – so that the subsidiary can pay for carriage in local currency – and to use a Malaysian carrier.

5 Budget

In view of the success of the company's other products – £8 million turnover in five years – cumulative sales of £5 million over three years can be expected, as follows:

	Year 1	Year 2	Year 3
sales (£ million)	0.75	1.75	2.50
cumulative	0.75	2.50	5.00

This would be accounted for as follows (assuming costs are 75 per cent, being lower than in the home market):

cumulative sales (£000s)	5,000
less costs (75%)	(3,750)
investment costs	(500)
cost of overseas operation	(500)
profit	250 (5%)

These figures are submitted without information on the cost of the local operation, and the sales target may have to be revised in order to cover the cost of this.

After initial costs have been recovered in Year 3, profitability will of course increase substantially.

Conclusion

More detailed proposals for this venture will be submitted after my visit to the area to obtain more detailed information, specifically:

1 Market size and potential.
2 Suitable location for venture – availability of labour, access to ports and so on.
3 Costs of the venture.
4 Local legislation affecting the plans.

The potential for the new truck is enormous, particularly in the fast-developing ASEAN region. The company should seize this opportunity to get established there as soon as possible. I am convinced that the investment will be well repaid.

Julia Spencer, MIEx(Grad)
8th June 1993

Note

This is a much more ambitious venture than either of those suggested previously, and we cannot be expected to give as much detail, or to have the necessary knowledge to make a full case. Some very sweeping assumptions have had to be made – in practice we could be way off course. **That does not matter**. The point is to demonstrate that we know how to balance the figures and make a convincing case. In real life we would get the information from sales records, published information, and other sources; here we just have to make sensible guesses. It is enough to show that we know what to do.

There are lots of conditions here – acceptability under local law, that the operation can be set up for the money available, and so on. Again, that doesn't matter. The important thing is to show we understand the issues, not to run away from them.

In pulling figures out of the air, we can at least make things easy by picking numbers which are easy to calculate. (The sales forecasts and presumed costs have been chosen just for that reason.) Many students make their tasks more difficult by working out detailed percentages. This is unnecessary – in the author's opinion, most of these questions can be done without a calculator.

The budget is very sketchy for this option, as there is little information on which to base figures – we cannot be expected to know the cost of a new company in Malaysia, for example. We have demonstrated that we know how to use figures and break even – that is enough. A different proposal, for example for direct export through a network of dealers, would have to be more detailed. For example:

Sales required (at 15% assumed profit) to recover £500,000

$$\text{Investment} = \frac{500,000 \times 100}{15} = \text{approximately 3.5 million.}$$

The sales forecast, based on company's growth to date, is £4-5 million by year 3. The following budget demonstrates that the objective can be achieved on cumulative turnover of £4 million, a conservative estimate:

	£000s
projected sales (cumulative)	4,000
manufacturing costs (70%)	(2,800)
	1,200
initial investment	(500)
	700

Selecting a Marketing Strategy: Case Study 2

	£000's	£000's
launch costs:		
publicity	10	
promotional video	10	
trade exhibitions (2)	50	
dealer training	5	
sales conference	10	
travel	5	
research	10	
		(100)
net profit		600 (15%)

Selecting a Marketing Strategy: Case Study 3

The third worked example comes from a very different question: Lines Ltd. Here we are dealing with a service industry –
interior design – and, in contrast to the previous question, have
a tiny budget of £20,000 with which to start exporting. With a
service industry selling can be difficult – though at least in this
case there are finished designs to reflect the quality of the service.

The Question

The company

Ten years ago a group of five interior designers, who had known
and worked with each other for several years, decided to form a
company called Lines Ltd. It was formed because each of them
had their own respective specialized skills, which were complementary to each other, and together enabled them to have a
competitive advantage over other interior designers, in that the
company was able to offer what was called its 'Full Service'.

The 'Full Service'

The 'Full Service' comes in two forms. For existing buildings, for example, large private houses or hotels, Lines will tear out the old fixtures and fittings and install new ones, according to an agreed design. For new houses or hotels, Lines will design and install the new interior. The important aspect is that, although subcontractors may be used, for example, carpenters, Lines oversee all of them, and guarantee to the customer that the job will be finished by the agreed date and be of satisfactory workmanship.

Current business

For the past three years, Lines' business has followed the same pattern. Contracts worth £1m, at an average contract size of £50,000, have come from refurbishing existing buildings, and contracts worth £2m, at an average contract size of £100,000, have come from new buildings. In both instances, 40 per cent of the business was for private houses and 60 per cent was for hotels. In all instances, Lines charged a 20 per cent commission fee on the contract, which gave the company an income of £600,000, which, after all expenses, left a net profit of £120,000.

The clients

Business is obtained from two sources: 50 per cent comes from word-of-mouth recommendations from past clients, both private individuals and hotel owners; and 50 per cent from public tenders, which are always issued by hotel owners.

Exports

Small contracts have been obtained in France, Spain, Italy and the United States, all by recommendations from previous clients, since many of their private clients have international contacts, while the hotel clients have recommended them to other hotels in the chain.

The Task

Lines have decided to expand exports and have agreed a target contract level of £500,000 for the next 12 months and have allocated £20,000 for the extra costs of obtaining this business. You have been asked to present a report which outlines your recommendations on what actions Lines should take to achieve the given objective. This must include your recommendations on the following topics:

1 Which market, or markets, should be developed, giving your reasons for your choice.
2 Outline marketing strategies for the chosen market, or markets.
3 Any specific problems, such as payment and insurance, and their proposed solutions, in the marketing of the 'full service' in the chosen market, or markets.
4 A quantified budget.

To Answer

Define the task

To obtain export contracts of £500,000 in next 12 months within a budget of £20,000.

Note that the company's average net profit at present is £120,000 out of £600,000, that is, 20 per cent; we are not told we are to achieve this.

Analyse the situation

1 The company is well-established, with a good reputation internationally.
2 There are good prospects for exporting; the company has secured contracts before purely on personal recommendations. With a systematic approach it should do far better. Personal recommendations are valuable in securing contracts.

3 The designers have all-round skills, including management. We do not know what sales or export skills, if any, they have (other than experience). They may need training if the company is to start exporting seriously.

4 Lines offer a Full Service and customer guarantee – this may give a competitive advantage.

5 There are already four countries – Italy, Spain, France and the United States – where Lines has a foothold. There may be even greater prospects elsewhere: rebuilding Kuwait; rapid economic development in the Gulf states (though if the designers are women, they might not easily do business there); the Far East; and so on.

6 There are also new opportunities in existing markets: the large British population in Spain, which might prefer to deal with British nationals; retirement and leisure developments in the United States, for example.

7 It seems there are no language problems – the company is clearly dealing with a cosmopolitan clientele. However, if it is to develop export in earnest, it should give thought to language training.

8 There are two big limitations: the budget (£20,000), and manpower. It is not clear whether anyone in the business has responsibility for sales and marketing; we certainly cannot afford to take on someone new on this budget. If the designers take on this responsibility, they will have less time to do their real work. And, given the personal nature of the service, there is a limit to how much more work the five designers can take on. (What happens if one of them is ill? The work cannot easily be delegated.) Consequently the company's ability to exploit export opportunities is limited and short-term.

9 The target contracts of £500,000 can be achieved with 10 refurbishing or five new contracts (assuming contract levels are the same as in the home market).

10 The new business represents an increase of one-sixth (£500,000 on £3m) – since only five designers are involved, this will probably tax their resources and capacity to the full. The budget of £20,000 is very modest (after the heady situation of Planos' £½ million).

11 The latter two factors suggest that long-term international involvement will be limited – unless the service can be franchised. (This gives low rewards, but great kudos.) However, achieving first-year income of £500,000 on signing fees and royalties alone will require contract levels far in excess of those which Lines has built up after 10 years.

12 The existing business handles four options: refurbishing or new contracts; and houses or hotels. With its limited resources it is best to concentrate on getting work from one sector only. (We do not know what opportunities exist in other sectors – for example the retirement market in the United States, where entire towns are built for the specific needs of senior citizens.)

13 The home market appears static. Is exporting a short-term response to this?

14 The present net profitability is 20 per cent (£120,000 on £600,000); apart from this there is little financial information, so no detailed analysis is possible. However, if the present commission and profitability levels are maintained – 20 per cent each – then the new venture will only succeed in breaking even (the profit on £500,000 being the same as the cost of the £20,000 investment in it). This seems strange.

Identify any gaps in information and decide what to do about them

There will be different technical standards to satisfy overseas, particularly in the United States where every state has different laws. In practice this is not likely to be a problem. The designers have worked abroad in the past, so we can assume they are competent to handle this.

There is no indication where the opportunities are. There are several ways of getting round this:

1 Draw on our own knowledge. If we know (or can guess) enough about a market to make a case for entering it, then that will be acceptable to the examiner.

2 Assume we have done what we would do in real life: make a decision based on the information to hand (for example sales records, information gained from field trips, desk research, a recommendation from an existing customer). The important thing is to demonstrate a reason for the decision. So, in the absence of hard information it is quite acceptable to say

'One of our customers in Italy is building three new hotels this year, and we have a good chance of obtaining a contract to design at least one of them. For this reason we should concentrate our export operation on the Italian market.' Or,

'Desk research has established that large hotel and leisure complexes are being built in Florida. Because we have successfully worked in Florida before, I recommend targeting this area as an export market.'

The important thing is to give good reasons for the recommendations.

Also, it is not clear what our part is in all this. Other questions say quite clearly (for example): 'You have been appointed Export Manager ...'. This question simply tells us to present a report – no more. The vagueness can be turned to our advantage, however. If we assume the role of Marketing Manager, with responsibility for the new operation, we can overcome some of the concerns highlighted earlier – lack of sales ability, demands on the designers' time, and so on.

Select market(s)

We have to name a country to which we are going to export systematically; in view of the small budget, and the importance of personal recommendations, it is best to go for a market where the company is already known: Spain, Italy, France or the United States. The United States is a large market, so any activity will be restricted to one or two states. The cost of travelling there may be prohibitive on such a small budget. The United States market is probably best left until Lines is better established.

A market sector within the country should also be identified, so that marketing efforts can be concentrated most effectively. There is a clear indication that we should be going for the hotel rather than the private house market:

1 It is easier to identify.
2 It is a larger market (giving 60 per cent of existing business)
3 Lines already knows the market.
4 There are better chances of repeat business, and hotels refurbish more often than individuals.

Select the product(s)

Lines offers two services – refurbishment of existing properties, and designing the interiors of new ones. They are clearly aimed at separate markets. In order to concentrate efforts where they will have most effect, we should go for one or the other. Again, there are clear indications that we should go for new contracts rather than refurbishing, since this brings in more money. Only five contracts will be needed to reach the target (assuming contract values remain the same as at present). Refurbishment contracts may also be more time-consuming because of the need to remove old fittings before work can start.

Decide on the distribution channel

In selling a service, particularly one as individual as design, most conventional distribution channels (for example agents or distributors) are not appropriate. What other options are available?

1 Direct selling, clearly, since this has worked in the past; since the company cannot afford an overseas sales office, contracts will have to be handled from the United Kingdom – another reason for choosing a market close at hand. (The designers are probably the best salesmen for the company; they will have to be involved with clients.)

2 Possibly piggybacking with architects who contract overseas; this would give economies of scale to both parties, and enlarge the range of services available, thereby making them more marketable. This would also require minimal effort from a company whose resources are clearly stretched already.

An ambitious and far-sighted solution to the lack of resources would be to franchise Lines' service overseas. Interestingly, the instructions specify achieving a **contract** level of £500,000; this would seem to preclude the franchising option. (Nonetheless, students have made a case for franchising, and passed.)

Plan promotion

With the given budget, little advertising is possible; but a very specific market (hotel chains with building programmes) can be reached more effectively by other means. Means of promotion which are suitable here are:

1 Personal selling – systematic approaches both to known contacts and identified prospects. (Desk research will have to be undertaken to identify decision-makers in hotel chains.) 'Influencers' – for example architects – may also be approached. At the same time the company must systematically tender for suitable projects (again, desk research will be needed to identify sources).
2 Public relations – inviting prospects (expenses paid) to a function in a Lines-decorated room to publicize their work; also, if funds permit, getting articles in the trade press.
3 A good portfolio to show customers.
4 Good quality brochures to convey the correct image of the company and its services.
5 Participating in a trade exhibition – if the company can afford it.

Decide on pricing

It seems that hotel contracts overseas earn the same as in the home market. With the weak pound, sterling is a selling point; but care must be taken not to underprice the service. For a product like this price is not critical. With the low margins on this venture, underpricing could be a serious mistake.

Establish any requirements for documentation, insurance and so on

In exporting a service there is no physical movement of goods, so there are no concerns about transport documents or customs procedures. If (as seems increasingly likely) Lines decides to target a European market, there will be free movement for its staff and their contractors to work within the European Community. So formalities will be minimal. The principal concerns will be to ensure a regular cash flow during the period of the contract, and see that there is adequate insurance.

Given that the designers all have different skills, the company would be extremely vulnerable if one of them were taken ill. Perhaps there should be key man insurance for this. Public liability insurance, especially in the United States, will be an extra cost.

Establish what the venture will cost

There is very little financial information and we are not asked to calculate profit. We do not know the fixed and variable costs – only that the present level of expenses is 80 per cent of income. Interestingly, if we assume this is maintained for the new business, we find that we only break even.

income (20% commission on £500,000)	£100
expenses (80%)	(80)
less launch expenses	(20)
net profit/loss	–

If we wish to keep the same level of profitability – 20 per cent of income – then expenses must be kept to 100-20-20 = 60 per cent. We are not told outright to make a profit, but this must be pointed out.

Estimate sales

No problem – we have already been given a target. But given that in the first year margins may be tight (see above), we should look to further development in the second year.

Finalize decisions

We have seen that a great deal points to a European market. There are three choices – Italy, Spain and France. The following recommendations assume Italy as a choice of market, although an equally good case could be made for either of the other two countries.

Write the report

Report to Managing Director

From Marketing Manager

Subject Recommendations for developing Lines Ltd export business

Introduction

Since my appointment I have been investigating opportunities for developing Lines Ltd's 'Full Service' business. It is clear that:

1 The UK market has been at same level for three years.
2 There are good opportunities for overseas business, particularly if pursued systematically.

However, it is equally clear that:

1 The company's ability to exploit overseas opportunities is limited by the amount of new work designers can take on.
2 Overseas contracts have to be handled from the United Kingdom office, since we cannot afford a local one at this stage.

As will be demonstrated below, the contract target of £500,000 for the first year's export business is barely profitable. The company must take a broader view if it is to succeed in export.

My strategy will therefore be to continue seeking international contracts in the short term (one year), as per my brief, and to establish the 'Full Service', but to franchise the service in selected overseas markets in the following year once the service has become better known.

The following recommendations deal only with plans for the first year.

1 Markets to be developed

For our first overseas operation we should enter Italy, for the following reasons:

1 Our knowledge of the hotel industry and contacts there inform us that hotel development is taking place.
2 Italy is a country which appreciates good design and where our service has already been well received.
3 There is easy access in case of problems, and the cost of travel is affordable.
4 Having worked there in the past, we already have sub-contractors competent to do the jobs.
5 Since Italy is a member of the European Community, there are minimal problems on payment, movement of staff and goods, and technical standards, since it is effectively now part of the domestic market.
6 Language has not hitherto been a problem, since most Italian hoteliers speak English and I speak sufficient Italian to

cope with informal business conversations. Since a high level of personal selling will be involved, some ability in the language of the market is essential.

Within Italy efforts should be concentrated on developing the hotel (rather than private house) market, since

1 it is easier to identify and target;
2 it is a larger market (60 per cent of existing business);
3 we already know the hotel industry; and
4 there are better chances of repeat business.

It is likely that we shall also continue to receive business from recommendations and repeat contracts. Any decision about how to handle this will have to be made in the light of available resources – given the limited extra work which the designers can handle, and our overall strategy as outlined above. No provision is made for such business in the sales forecast.

2 Outline marketing strategies for the chosen market

Product
Lines should offer only its 'Full Service' for new interiors, since these contracts are on average twice the value of refurbishment.

Price
My proposals assume charging the same price in Italy as for a contract in the United Kingdom, and the budget has been submitted on this basis. There may however be a case for charging higher prices:

1 Good design is not price-sensitive.
2 Expenses will have to be contained in order to maintain profit levels.
3 Quoting a higher price gives greater flexibility, for example in allowing prompt payment discounts (which may be a factor in Italy).

4 A higher price will help position Lines as a provider of quality service.

Place

Because the individual nature of design needs a high degree of personal involvement, direct selling is the best way of achieving sales. Unfortunately our budget is not large enough to set up a sales office in Italy, but the market is close enough to be handled from the United Kingdom. Where it is necessary to meet customers in Italy, we should hire a room decorated by Lines in which to entertain them. I shall handle initial approaches myself but the designers should be involved in negotiations from an early stage, and time must be scheduled into their workload for this.

Promotion

My sales drive will be twofold: direct approaches to named buyers in the hotel business; and systematic monitoring of tenders to ensure that Lines responds to all suitable opportunities.

As mentioned above, personal approaches will be most effective in securing sales. My first task will be to build up a list of prospective customers in the Italian hotel business, compiled from existing records, personal recommendations, and trade directories. We must understand the complete buying process and identify not just the decision-makers, but also 'influencers', for example architects. Prospects should be approached individually on a systematic basis to establish whether there is any possibility of work.

Sales efforts will be supplemented by other promotion:

1 Good quality brochures to send prospects after the initial approach.
2 Hospitality at premises decorated by us.
3 A good portfolio of work, showing before and after pictures, with specifications such as budgets and timescale demonstrating that we can work to targets and details of any awards, testimonials from satisfied customers, and press reports. The portfolio should be presented in Italian and English, but in

such a way that it can easily be adapted to other languages later.

4 Publicity in the hotel trade press.

5 If resources permit, participation in a trade exhibition.

I am travelling to Milan (the centre of the Italian advertising industry) next month to appoint an agency to handle PR, brochures and the portfolio, and exhibition if required. At the same time I shall undertake any necessary desk research locally. While on the spot I also intend to make preliminary approaches to identified prospects in the hotel industry.

3 Specific problems such as payment and insurance

With the Single European Market no formalities are necessary for us to enter Italy or work there, nor are there any customs restrictions on equipment we need to take into the country. As we have worked in Italy before we are conversant with the appropriate regulations on public liability, employment law and technical standards, and already have the necessary insurance cover to meet these. (Our staff will be covered by our own insurance policy while working, but we will require evidence from our subcontractors that they too have adequate cover.) In view of the personal and specialized nature of the design service, the demands on the designers' time, and the fact that design cannot easily be delegated, the company should take out key man insurance for its designers at this stage.

In order to ensure a steady flow of income, contracts should provide for stage payments from signing of the contract until the work is completed. If dealing with new customers, a credit check should be taken on them before signing the contract. In the past we have experienced slow payment from Italy and in view of this prompt payment discounts should be offered (see comment above on pricing). Payment may be made through the SWIFT system.

4 Budget

The following budget assumes five contracts, each worth £100,000, for new hotels. It does not allow for any work obtained as a result of personal recommendations or repeat business from old customers.

No information is available about present costs, but these should be established as a matter of urgency. In order to maintain the company's usual profit level of 20 per cent, first year expenses will have to be kept to 60 per cent of income to allow for the extra cost (£20,000) of the new export venture. The following assumes that this is possible.

Figures are given in £000s, although customers should be invoiced in lire if they prefer this. No allowance is made for currency fluctuations.

income (20% commission on 500)		100
expenses (60%)		(60)
less launch expenses:		
portfolio	2	
translation	1	
publicity	5	
hospitality	5	
travel	4	
hire of rooms	3	(20)
net profit		20

Desk research and direct selling are to be undertaken by me and so at no extra cost to the company.

Julia Spencer,
Export Manager.

Note

We are assuming here that the company is exporting as an alternative to a static home market, where sales have been the same for three years. This is a quite different approach from the previous question, where the export operation was seen as a way of recouping the very heavy development costs, and the company clearly had long-term export plans.

You have been warned against suggesting too much research. In this case it is a natural starting-point for building up a list of prospects; we cannot proceed without it.

There is no harm in mentioning broader issues such as long-term prospects; it shows you can think strategically.

Inventing something (that is, the market prospects in Italy) from our own records to back up our case is acceptable; it is important to give reasons. Research should in any case start in the company itself.

Similarly, you can solve a problem by stating you speak the language; this is the sort of factor which, in real life, might well influence a decision on market entry.

General Advice

After this detailed analysis, all that remains is to give some general advice on answering the Section A question:

1   Stick to the format of the question – if it is divided into sections, 1, 2, 3, 4, 5 (or a, b, c, d, e) use those same sections in the answer.
2   Write in report, not essay, form.
3   Read the instructions.
4   Don't equate promotion just with advertising. Other forms of promotion – personal selling, direct mail, publicity, trade fairs, point-of-sale – can be far more effective.
5   Be consistent; don't suggest promoting an industrial product in a consumer medium like television, for example.
6   Be realistic: don't expect to make £3 million profit or to enter 12 markets in your first year. Other suggestions have been to set up, simultaneously, a Far East manufacturing operation, a European Community distribution centre, and a United States agency, all in the first year. While each of these options may be perfectly valid, attempting three such

disparate operations in a short period, with limited export experience and resources, is (in the words of one examiner's report) a marketing headache.

7 Always give reasons for what you suggest.
8 State your assumptions, and how they are arrived at.
9 Remember your turnover must cover costs (fixed plus variable, or direct plus indirect, depending on how the question is phrased) and leave something over for profit. (If in doubt about the meaning of financial terms, consult the companion volume in this series, *Principles of Management in Export.*)
10 Show your profit, and how it is arrived at.
11 Don't assume that market conditions are the same overseas as in the home market. Pricing is a case in point. If the export market is an affluent one, then it can afford to pay – especially for a quality product. (A convincing case has been made for tripling the price of designer clothes in Italy, in order to give them status in a fashion-conscious market.) In other markets you may have to reduce the selling price in order to secure a sale. Some distribution channels in the domestic market – department stores, DIY chains and so on – simply do not exist in others. And there may be applications for a product which do not exist in the home market. Also, opportunities are different overseas. For the Lines designers, to concentrate in the United States on the hotel market would be to overlook the greater opportunities there for building entire retirement towns. And so on.
12 Above all, establish the financial objective and stick to it.

A further example of a Section A question is now given for further practice.

The Question

Introduction

Jim Cook, an electronics engineer, and Ian Howard, a mechanical engineer, formed a company, C & H Ltd, about 10 years ago, to manufacture and market to garages engine tuning equipment. Since then, they have built up the company to be one of the leading suppliers of specialist garage equipment for tuning high performance car engines. The company now has a turnover of £1m, apart from the product described below.

The product

Three years ago, after considerable market research, research and development and deliberation, C & H launched a machine, based on electronics, which enabled any reasonably competent person to tune a car engine and to check the exhaust emissions, at the same time.

It was designed in a modular form. Hence, the basic machine (model A) was sold to large DIY stores for £200, to be sold at £300 to private individuals. Model B was sold to garage equipment wholesalers for £500, who sold it for £750, either to small garages or to individuals, who installed it in a van and visited people's homes. Model C was sold for £2,000 direct to garages, normally those which specialized in car engine tuning and carried out government specified tests on older cars.

It was an immediate success, especially Model A, because, C & H discovered, individuals saw it as a good investment which would cut the costs of preparing their cars for the increasingly rigorous, and expensive, government specified tests for any car over three years old. Sales were, in fact, in the ratio of 3 Model A to 2 Model B and 1 Model C, and the total net sales last year were £576,000.

Exports

C & H have received orders from overseas for the machines and last year net sales were £72,000. The prices used were the net prices in the United Kingdom and the ratio of model sales was the same as the United Kingdom as well. Because of the modular design, variable costs of each model were 50% of the net selling price and, when fixed costs had been covered, each model had a net profitability of 15 per cent.

The sales were made to continental Europe, the United States and Scandinavia in approximately equal proportions.

C & H have already had offers from companies overseas to act as agents, distributors and, in one case, a request to manufacture it under licence in the United States.

The Task

You have been appointed Export Manager with the specific brief to exploit the product's success as quickly as possible, before a competitive machine is launched. (C & H already have a more sophisticated machine under development.) You have been given a budget of £54,000 to cover the extra costs of marketing and setting up the channels of distribution overseas. C & H expect to recover the budget within 12 months of the start of the export operation.

In the meantime, you are to present an initial report which outlines your recommendations on the actions to be taken to achieve the given objective. This report must include your recommendations on the following points:

1 Which market, or markets, should be developed, giving reasons for your choice.
2 Outline marketing strategies for the chosen market, or markets.
3 Any problems, and their solutions, regarding physical distribution, documentation, payment, and so on.
4 A quantified budget.

4

World Markets

This chapter considers the characteristics of the world's major markets and market groupings and their effect on the United Kingdom's export trade, along with the factors to consider in identifying export markets, and some of the events currently affecting world trade. Readers are advised to keep up to date with developments; in a rapidly changing world, some information is likely to be out of date by the time the book is published. An understanding of the world economic environment is the basis for any decision on market entry, and is therefore dealt with in some detail.

Most trade groupings mentioned below are organized on a geographical basis, though some, such as the Gulf Cooperation Council, have been formed for political or ideological reasons. In considering trade groupings it is useful to distinguish between:

1 A free trade area – a group of countries having common internal tariffs.
2 A customs union – countries sharing common internal and external tariffs, such as Switzerland and Liechtenstein.
3 A common market – a group of countries having common tariffs and a free flow of capital, people and goods between countries.

It is also worthy of note that not all the associations discussed have been equally successful. Although in some groups members

have developed complementary rather than competing industries – this was an objective of the now-disbanded COMECON –
in many cases the economies of neighbouring countries have
been too similar to make much trade feasible. The ALADI (Latin
American Free Trade Association) countries, for example, are
more dependent on non-members - notably the United States
for manufactured goods and machinery – than on each other.
Other groups have had limited success because of political
differences between members, instability in member states, or
simply lack of commitment.

Western Europe

The European Community (EC) – now known, since the
ratification of the Maastricht treaty, as the European Union (EU)
– is one of the world's three largest markets (along with the
United States and Japan). The Single European Market came
into being on 1 January 1993 and abolished all controls
between the 12 European Community member states: the United
Kingdom, Ireland, France, Germany, Belgium, Netherlands,
Denmark, Luxembourg, Italy, Spain, Portugal and Greece. The
Single Market has brought about common technical standards,
uniform documentation procedures and external customs tariff;
similar business standards – for example, open account terms
are expected – the deregulation of transport (which has opened
domestic routes to carriers from other EC member states), and
cross-border tendering for major contracts.

A common currency (the European Currency Unit, or ECU)
already exists on paper and is planned to become available for
circulation once a European Central Bank has been set up.

An affluent market of over 300 million people, the Market is
characterized by a large industrial sector, dependence on imports of fuel and raw materials, growing service industries, and
a highly-protected, over-producing agricultural sector.

The UK's entry to the European Community had a profound
effect on her trading patterns, coming as it did at a time when
her traditional markets in the Commonwealth were also seeking new trading partners. Until the 1950s, the UK supplied

manufactured goods to developing nations, particularly former colonies, in exchange for raw materials. As these countries gained independence they started to develop their own industries and also look for new trading relationships, so the UK no longer had easy markets for her products. When the UK joined the Community, she increased trade with her European partners to the further detriment of Commonwealth partners. Entry into the European Community also opened the country up to more competition, notably from newly-industrialized countries like Italy with more modern and competitive industries, and industries subsidized by foreign governments, for example Dutch greenhouse produce which benefits from cheap heating. The UK has been criticized for her failure to compete on non-price factors such as quality, after-sales and delivery. The country is now exporting fewer finished goods to developing countries and is exporting instead knowhow through licensing arrangements or joint ventures.

The European Union has an agreement (known as the Lome convention) with a number of ACP (African, Caribbean and Pacific) states – most of them former colonies – to encourage development and give those countries easy access to Community markets.

The success of the European Community stimulated the formation of a number of other regional trade blocs, some of which are discussed below.

The European Free Trade Association (EFTA) – Iceland, Austria, Switzerland, Liechtenstein, Norway, Sweden and Finland – has a close relationship with the Community; common documentation and minimal formalities exist between the two blocs. A new European Economic Area (EEA) was intended to unite the Community and the Free Trade Area (other than Switzerland) on 1st July 1993; while Austria, Sweden, Finland and Norway are negotiating to join the Community.

Eastern Europe

At the time of writing, the area is in the throes of a profound reorientation following the collapse of Communism, the dismantling of the Soviet Union, the disintegration of Comecon and the emergence of newly-independent states such as Estonia, the Slovak Republic and Croatia. Much of Eastern Europe is in transition to market economies, while former state-run industries are being privatized and streamlined. This is providing opportunities for exports of western knowhow and technology, and western countries are investing heavily in the region. Aid programmes are also being funded by the EBRD (the European Bank for Reconstruction and Development) and western governments.

Some former Comecon countries (Czech and Slovak Republics, Poland) have become associate members of the European Community, and others (Bulgaria and Romania) are negotiating to do the same.

Meanwhile the former Soviet republics (other than the Baltic states and Georgia) have grouped into a Community of Independent States (CIS). The countries are still largely interdependent, but there is some disagreement over the degree to which their economies and infrastructure should be integrated. Most former Soviet republics have preserved the rouble as their currency, although there have been concerns that Russia is trying to control the so-called rouble zone. The CIS (the Community of Independent States) has been discussing a common pricing policy (modelled on OPEC, the Organization of Petroleum Exporting Nations) for energy and other key commodities. A common market of Central Asian (formerly Soviet) states has been proposed. Russia and its neighbours are in transition to market economies, and further changes can be expected in the area.

North America

The area is of course dominated by the United States – a market of 250 million people which produces one quarter of the world's output.

Despite high productivity, agricultural production is contracting, as are the defence and car industries, but there are growing new industries: computers, aerospace and pharmaceuticals. There are 50 states, each with different sets of laws (in addition to federal ones). The west and south-west of the country are particularly strong economically, with California and Texas the most important manufacturing states (by value).

United States exports became uncompetitive in the mid 1980s because of the rise in the value of the dollar; the country has had a trade deficit since 1985 and is dependent on oil imports despite large domestic production.

By contrast, Canada, the world's second largest country in area, is a large exporter of oil, gas and minerals and has one of the lowest population densities, with much of the country uninhabitable or unsuitable for cultivation. A large proportion of the population live within 100 miles of the border, and most of the country's exports now go to the United States. Like that country, Canada has been hit by worldwide surpluses in agriculture.

Until the GATT agreement of December 1993, the United States was at variance with the European Community over the Community's Common Agricultural Policy (CAP) subsidies, which hit US agricultural exports. It was largely as a result of this that the North American Free Trade Area (NAFTA), consisting of Canada, Mexico and the US, was formed. This is likely to increase the country's investment and manufacturing in Mexico, although there are fears in the United States that this will be tantamount to exporting jobs.

Central and Latin America

Most countries in the Americas are heavily dependent on trade with the United States, and several (Mexico, Brazil, Argentina and Venezuela) are struggling to service large debts incurred in the 1980s. There have been a number of schemes to reschedule these, hampered by severe inflation (particularly in Brazil) and political instability. Despite extremes of poverty and wealth, fast-growing population and massive external debt, Brazil has the ninth largest economy in the world in terms of gross domestic product (1989) and contains half the population of South America. In the past, the UK made large loans to central and south American countries for the purchase of British manufactured goods, but collapses of economies there meant debts had to be written off and trade with the area has suffered as a result.

The major market groupings in the area are:

1 ALADI (Latin American Integration Association, formerly LAFTA) – 10 Latin American countries, divided into most developed (Brazil, Argentina), intermediate (Venezuela, Chile), and least developed (Bolivia, Paraguay), the latter having special preferences. It also has external agreements and aims for cooperation in tourism, culture, environment and other activities. However, the countries are more dependent on outside markets than each other, and smaller groupings within the region have been formed, notably the Andean Common Market (ANCOM) consisting of Bolivia, Colombia, Ecuador, Peru, and Venezuela. Mercosul or Mercosur, formed in 1991 between Brazil, Paraguay, Uruguay and Argentina, has been successful in boosting trade in the area by cutting tariffs. Mexico, Venezuela and Colombia have also been discussing a new free trade zone, though it is not clear how this will affect NAFTA.
2 CARICOM – the Caribbean Community and Common Market which co-ordinates customs, fiscal and economic policies, and encourages local industry.
3 The Central American Common Market (CACM) – formed to liberalize trade, but has been hampered by internal supply problems and the external dependence of the economies.

Africa

The Arab countries of North Africa are divided on the one hand into the Maghreb (the west) – Algeria, Morocco and Tunisia, former French colonies with strong ties with Europe, and agriculture-based economies – and, on the other hand, Egypt and Libya, which are more closely aligned with the Middle East. An attempt was made to create a Maghreb customs union but without success.

In West Africa, ECOWAS (Economic Area of West African States) is an association of developing and mainly agricultural economies, formed for economic, social and cultural cooperation, and with a fund to help development in poorer states. It is dominated by oil-rich Nigeria, a country of over 100 million people, with a large foreign debt because of the fall in oil prices. Again, the countries' economies are too similar to satisfy each others' needs. ECOWAS overlaps to some extent with the Communauté Economique de l'Afrique de l'Ouest (CEAO), consisting of the French-speaking west African territories. There is also a Franc Zone, mainly comprising former French colonies, which have a freely convertible currency linked to the French franc.

Further south, there is the Preferential Trade Area for Eastern and Southern Africa (PTA), consisting of 17 members including Kenya, Malawi, Somalia, Tanzania, Zambia and Zimbabwe. Meanwhile South Africa is re-emerging after a period of isolation and is developing new trading partners.

Primarily producers of raw materials (both agricultural and mineral), many African countries are dependent on a single commodity (Zambia on copper, Guinea on bauxite). Population growth in much of the continent has been greater than the countries' ability to sustain it, so economic development has been slow. There is a need for capital projects and industrial goods to develop the economic infrastructure, but often little foreign exchange to pay for them (unless funded by overseas aid programmes). In the past, the UK supplied former colonies in Africa with manufactured goods in exchange for raw materials. These countries are increasingly manufacturing their own products and seeking new trading partners, while the UK is buying more from the European Community instead. Nigeria in particular was a major customer for British goods during the oil boom, but since the collapse of oil prices trade has fallen dramatically.

Middle East

The area is dominated by the Arab states – over 20 countries with 200 million inhabitants, and a wide range of races and political systems and factions, ranging from the strict Moslem and anti-Communist state of Saudi Arabia to the liberal and cosmopolitan Gulf states. The unifying factor is the Arabic language, which varies enormously from one part of the world to another.

Some of the Middle Eastern economies – Iraq, Iran, Saudi Arabia – are dependent on oil for over 80 per cent of their exports. The oil-rich Gulf States developed their industries and infrastructure in the late 1970s to lessen their dependence on oil, and opened up the area as a major market. During the war between Iran and Iraq the Gulf Cooperation Council was formed to protect trade in the Gulf. This has achieved some cooperation in customs duty and insurance regulations, but little in the way of sharing resources which at the moment are duplicated between the states. The Council also provides economic aid to the poorer, non-oil producing states of the Middle East and north Africa, although recently it has also invested further afield.

Other blocs within the region are the Arab League, formed to foster cooperation between Arab states, but which disagreed over recognition of Israel and intervention after the invasion of Kuwait; and OAPEC, the Organisation of Arab Petroleum Exporting Countries, a producer cartel formed to encourage cooperation and safeguard members' interests. Some alliances now operate more on a geographical basis – the Red Sea region, North Africa, the Gulf, the Levant (Syria, Jordan, Lebanon) and the Maghreb. It is not clear whether there will be any re-alignment between the Moslem republics of the former Soviet Union, still economically dependent on Russia, and its southern neighbours.

Middle Eastern countries of course also dominate OPEC, the Organisation of Petroleum Exporting Countries, which in 1973 raised oil prices, hitting the United Kingdom (as an oil importer) and in turn making British manufactured goods uncompetitive.

Far East and the Pacific Rim

The area is dominated by Japan, a country which produces one tenth of the world's gross national product but has only 3 per cent of the world's population on 0.3 per cent of the world's land, most of the country being uninhabitable.

Japan is heavily dependent on imports for food, energy and raw materials. Nonetheless, it has enormous trade surpluses, imports being one quarter less than its exports. It is a large importer, however, of services. In recent years there has been much international pressure on Japan to reduce its trade surplus by importing more – although Japan has resisted this.

The business environment in Japan is very formal and differs in many ways from that in the west. With a paternalistic society and management, there is also a tradition of conformism, so action is seen to be taken by groups, not individuals. Decisions are made on the basis of long-term relationships and strategy, not short-term profit. Government and business are closely allied, and there is heavy interdependence between the corporate sector and the small firms which service it. The large trading corporations (sogo shosha) are particularly important; nine of them control 50-60 per cent of Japan's external trade. The keiretsu, large groups of companies based round a major bank or trading company and with their own network of manufacturing and distribution companies, make market entry difficult for foreign companies. There is also a complex and inefficient multi-stage distribution network. Other problems faced by exporters are the need to minimize stock (because of the cost of warehousing) at the same time as ensuring prompt delivery and a long-term relationship. For this reason the foreign companies which succeed in the market are usually those which have joint ventures with a Japanese partner, thereby easing the problems of language, distribution and bureaucracy.

Japan is a country of discriminating consumers, expecting high standards of value and service, and who will pay high prices for luxury foreign imports. Its rapid industrial development after the Second World War has made it increasingly competitive in international trade; British industries such as motorcycle and car manufacturing and electronics have been particularly affected. Japanese companies now have subsidiaries all over the world, having established them in the European Community often ahead of other European countries.

Traditionally the United States, the Far East and Australia have been seen as separate markets, but in recent years there has been increasing interdependence in the countries of the Pacific Rim (also known as the Pacific Basin), the area which includes Japan, the western United States, the industrializing countries of the Association of South East Asian Nations (ASEAN), South Korea, Hong Kong and Taiwan, as well as Australia and New Zealand; there is comparatively little trade, at present, with South America. Australia and New Zealand are particularly important to Japan as markets for its manufactured goods and as sources of minerals and foodstuffs. At the same time, there is heavy Japanese investment in the western states of the United States. North American trade with Asia now exceeds that with Europe, and the heaviest flow of container traffic in the world is across the Pacific.

The newly industrializing countries of Asia, once dismissed for copying western ideas, have become serious competitors because of their low manufacturing costs and modern industries. They are growing rapidly, with rising levels of consumption, self-sufficiency in basic goods and many natural resources. The area is also noted for a high level of trade in counterfeit goods. It is a more heterogeneous region than (for example) Europe and there is considerable scope for further development. China, in particular, is emerging as a world market, with much international investment being made in the country. At present, much of its trade is done through Hong Kong, though it is uncertain how this will continue after the territory reverts to China in 1997.

The major trading bloc in the Pacific Rim is the Association of South East Asian Nations (ASEAN), whose declared objective is also to cooperate in social, cultural, educational and other fields. Consisting of Malaysia, Singapore, Thailand, Indonesia and the Philippines, ASEAN has been one of the more successful organizations of its type and has recently signed a cooperation treaty with Vietnam and Laos.

Another grouping in the area is the Asian Pacific Economic Cooperation (APEC) – an Australian initiative aimed primarily at establishing cooperation between the governments of the ASEAN countries and Australia, New Zealand, Japan, Canada, South Korea and the United States. Although the countries agreed in 1990 to reduce trade barriers, at present little has been achieved. Meanwhile Japan, which has hitherto remained apart from any major trading bloc, has proposed a new East Asian Economic Caucus (a free trade area) to balance NAFTA and the European Community.

Australasia

Despite its size, Australia is an area which is highly urbanized and enjoys a high standard of living, good transport and communications as well as a growing manufacturing base. Producers mainly of primary products (agricultural and mineral), Australia and New Zealand have been affected by fluctuating prices and restricted access to the British market since its entry to the European Community, and are now developing trading relationships with other partners. Both countries are now trading more with Japan than with the UK. The area is heavily interdependent with other countries of the Pacific Rim, including the United States.. Australia is also a founder member of the Cairns group, an association of agricultural exporters which includes Canada and twelve predominantly Asian and Latin American countries. The group was formed to press for wider markets for agricultural products, and was instrumental in getting agriculture on the agenda of the GATT talks which were concluded in December 1993.

Indian Subcontinent

India, Pakistan, Bangladesh and Sri Lanka are industrializing countries with rising levels of consumption, growing middle classes, and increasing self-sufficiency in food and basic goods. They are also experiencing rapid population growth and economic problems, particularly balance of payment difficulties. The size of the market – 800 million people in India alone – makes it attractive to foreign companies, although in India government limits on foreign investment have restricted the options for market entry. India is the world's tenth most industrialized nation, although both Pakistan and Sri Lanka have a higher per capita output. India has a tradition of non-alignment, and does not belong to any trading blocs. As can be expected in a region of this size, a diversity of cultures, religions and languages have to be taken into account in dealing with the area.

Natural Trade Groupings

Despite the existence of so many trading blocs, geographical proximity does not necessarily mean cooperation, as in the case of Cuba and the United States or, until recently, South Africa and her neighbours. Adjacent countries often have similar economies and hence a limited ability to trade with each other. All over the world there are examples of overlapping language, culture, communications, and tastes, where political and racial boundaries do not coincide. The former West Germany was said to have eight distinct marketing regions in which tastes and culture overlapped to a large degree with those of neighbouring countries.

The recognition that many markets transcend national boundaries has given rise to the concept of the total market – selling the same product worldwide (changing only the language on the packaging), and ignoring differences between countries. This in turn has led to the development of global products, which can be marketed in as many countries as possible: colour film, car hire services and hotels are examples of this. Both Ford and General Motors have attempted to develop world cars; pop music and jeans have universal appeal to young people; and Coca-Cola is often quoted as an example of a global brand (though its Indian rival has seriously challenged it in some markets). Some multinationals have taken global arrangements a step further by producing components in different markets and then assembling them in different countries in order to produce something which is truly international. This also gives them the advantage of flexibility; if there are problems at one plant, they can switch production to a different place. Products which have become industry standards are further examples of global products – the IBM personal computer or, in the military sphere, the NATO sweater which is worn by most of the armed forces of Europe.

It is worth remembering that a product is not just a physical product but incorporates intangible benefits such as brand, guarantee, availability of spare parts and consumables, service and other factors which give it a competitive edge. Development of a global product can be impeded by the fact that it is not always possible to offer the same level of service worldwide.

World Economic Environment

We shall now look at some of the factors which influence the selection of export markets, and the demand for products there. Some of the factors will also mean product modification – for cultural or racial differences, legal requirements, tariffs, nationalism, technical reasons, taxation or climate – to ensure success. Readers will no doubt be able to think of their own examples.

Demographic

The size, location and concentration of population give an indication of a market's potential. Population factors vary greatly between countries and even in different parts of the same market. Approximately half the population of the world lives in six countries: China, India, the United States, Indonesia, Japan and Brazil. In contrast Canada is sparsely populated, except along its border with the United States. Growing populations in developing countries, such as Brazil and parts of Africa, can mean a high demand for things but decreasing resources to pay for them. Western Europe, which is affluent and densely populated, has low population growth and consequently offers limited prospects for market expansion. Within each country there are market segments differentiated by such factors as age, lifestyle, spending power and education. Longer life expectancy and a falling birthrate in the developed countries have led to older populations in western Europe and North America where entire towns may be retirement areas. As a result, the demand is for products suitable for affluent, older people. In contrast, the high proportion of under-20-year-olds in Singapore means there will be a need for educational services and children's clothes and toys. The increase in single person households in developed countries has given rise to products developed specifically for this market, such as single portion meals. Minority groups within a country can constitute a significant market for specialist or upmarket goods, and foreigners are actually in a majority in some of the Gulf states which have only small indigenous populations.

Economic

The OECD (Organisation for Economic Cooperation and Development) recognises five stages in countries' economic development:

1 industrialized such as the United States, Germany, the United Kingdom, and Japan;
2 semi-industrial: Australia, South Africa;
3 newly-industrializing countries (NICs): Greece, Brazil, and Taiwan;
4 developing: Zimbabwe, Pakistan;
5 less developed: Burkina Faso.

All of these stages have characteristics which will affect the demand for a company's product. For example, bicycles are a means of transport in China and parts of Africa. In developed countries, where the use of cars is commonplace, bicycles are a leisure product with all manner of special clothes and accessories to go with them. In affluent western societies, sophisticated healthcare is needed for cancer and other 'western' diseases, whereas developing societies need a far more basic service aimed at reducing infant mortality and malnutrition.

Exporters considering entering a market will need to think about the following factors.

Communications
Does the country have reliable internal and international telephone, postal and fax services? In one African country, communication was so poor that the only way to send a message from one part of the country to another was to put someone on a plane to deliver the message personally. Local media may be merely government propaganda channels, and inappropriate for advertising.

Transport systems
Whether it is possible to get the goods to the markets safely and efficiently.

Distribution channels
These may be totally different from those in the home market. In Switzerland, 70 per cent of food distribution is in the hands of two companies; in Italy, salt (a state monopoly) can only be bought at tobacconists.

Location of markets
In Australia, most engineering is in the south-east of the country, but consumers are widely dispersed; whereas more than half of all the United States' industrial buyers are concentrated in seven of the 50 states.

Income
Both personal (per capita) and national (GNP); sometimes there are uneven spreads of wealth which include a rich few, an impoverished majority and a small middle class; hence the demand is for luxury items for the few and basics for the majority. This is a characteristic of many developing countries. Also the availability of foreign exchange to pay for goods, or materials to barter for them, is an important factor.

Existence of business infrastructure
Such as banking systems.

Government spending
This affects demand for health services, defence, and education.

Dependence on one or two commodities such as Zambia on copper, can make a country vulnerable to price changes.

Local industries which have to buy machinery from other countries

Natural resources

The availability and exploitability of a country's raw materials will determine both its needs and its ability to pay for them. In Hong Kong even drinking water has to be imported; in other countries natural resources such as fuel provide the money to pay for imported goods. The terrain, too, affects the availability of products – mountains form natural barriers while rivers can provide transport right to the centre of a continent, such as the St Lawrence Seaway between Canada and the United States, and the Amazon in Brazil. Transport to landlocked countries gives particular problems. Labour is a major export from some countries, which depend on income from their nationals working abroad, and a major cost in others. Climate is another factor to consider. It influences lifestyle and hence the goods which will be in demand; it can also damage goods which can need special packing or modification before they can be sold.

Technological

The level of development of a country (remembering that development can be an emotive word) will also affect a country's needs in various ways such as the availability of power to operate machines and the degree of automation. Some companies have been developing intermediate technology appropriate to the needs of developing countries, recognizing that more sophisticated machines are not suitable and utilizing new technology with existing products – Letraset is now available on computer for use with desk-top publishing programs. Exporters also need to be aware of national technical standards which have to be complied with – DIN in Germany, ASA in the United States, BS in the UK, and EN in the European Community. It is worth mentioning that a country's wealth is not necessarily a measure of its technological advancement; developing countries have managed to install new colour television networks despite heavy dependence on foreign aid.

Political and legal

This covers a host of factors such as the attitudes of government which may encourage, restrict or prohibit foreign trade, particularly in order to protect local industries. Brazil has a policy of prohibiting imports unless there is no 'national similar' whereas India, Nigeria and Saudi Arabia all have limits on the amount of foreign investment which can be brought into the country. Legislation covering a wide range of subjects such as advertising practices, food and drug regulations, agency law, consumer protection, taxation, company formation and price maintenance, can all affect a company's prospects in a market. Exporters to the United States need to satisfy both federal laws and those of whatever states they operate in. There are also countries which lack the standards other markets take for granted. As a result, western companies have been criticized for selling allegedly sub-standard foods and drugs to developing countries. Bureaucratic delays are usually associated with developing countries, but have also been felt closer to home, such as the French government's requirement for imported video recorders to be processed through a small inland customs post, thereby closing the market to Japanese imports. Even the materials which exporters use for packaging their goods are subject to legal restrictions (straw is banned in Australia, for example); other materials may be subject to import duty. The volatility of governments, their currencies and their policies should also be considered.

Cultural

As indicated already, political boundaries rarely coincide with racial or linguistic ones: the Italian-speaking part of Switzerland, Swedish-speaking Finns, the former Yugoslavia, Belgium and much of Africa are examples of this. Regional identities can be stronger than national ones – some newspapers in Germany and Italy have regional rather than national circulation. Racial and linguistic antipathies can be particularly strong: in parts of Africa people of one tribe will not do business with another.

Tastes are another difference to take into account: fat women are considered beautiful in Africa, unlike Europe and the United States. When exported, clothes have to be altered to suit local sizes, preferences and tastes.

Social factors, such as the role of women, have far-reaching effects on the way a company can operate overseas. In many cultures it will be difficult to conduct market research among women, or impractical to send a woman manager to conduct business negotiations.

Religious beliefs must be taken into account when assessing an export market as religion has its own taboos: the cow is sacred to Hindus; Muslims and Jews avoid pork; and cookery books destined for Saudi Arabia need to avoid any recipes calling for the use of alcohol. However, there are reports that a manufacturer of tinsel Christmas trees sold them in Saudi Arabia with great success (as Haj trees!).

Care also has to be taken not to offend national pride, for instance by using packaging the colour of the national flag. Different business practices abound: in some countries bribery and corruption are the accepted way of doing business, even where this is officially illegal.

GATT

Finally, no survey of world trade would be complete without mention of the General Agreement on Tariffs and Trade (GATT), established in 1949 to liberalize world trade, and with over 100 countries now participating.

The most recent (Uruguay) round of talks will probably be remembered for the long dispute between the European Community and the United States. Previous rounds of GATT talks had succeeded in reducing tariffs on manufactured goods, but not on agricultural products, which remained subject to protectionist measures. In particular, export subsidies for European farm produce had resulted in overproduction and also made agricultural exports from other countries, particularly the United States and north Africa, uncompetitive. Under pressure from the US and the Cairns Group, the Uruguay Round discussed agriculture for the first time. The farm subsidy issue led to a long conflict between the United States and Europe, and there was a long deadlock in which numerous deadlines were missed. However, an agreement was finally reached at the end of 1993. Under this the EC agreed to reduce farm subsidies over a six year period, while the US and EC agreed to cut tariffs on each other's products by over 50 per cent. The agreement also made it easier for developing countries to sell their produce overseas.

The Uruguay Round also considered, for the first time, international trade in services – audiovisual, maritime, financial and others. The new agreement provides for some deregulation in trade in services, as well as international recognition of intellectual property (trademarks, patents and copyrights). However, the US failed in its attempt to win better access to the EC film and TV market, which the Europeans opposed in order to protect their own industries; it is possible that quotas on the content of cable and satellite programmes may now be imposed as a result.

The agreement immediately brought down many trade barriers, with large tariff cuts, especially in previously protected Latin American and Asian markets. It also provided for the gradual phasing out of non-tariff barriers (quotas, local content requirement) and the Multifibre Agreement. A new Multilateral Trade Organisation is to be set up to police and enforce the agreement, which is expected to stimulate enormous growth in international trade.

Questions for Discussion

1 What opportunities are presented by the recent changes in Eastern Europe to British exporters and how can exporters capitalize on these opportunities?

2 In what way do you think that the Single European Act of 1992 will affect sales of British goods to other European Community countries?

3 To what extent can a British manufacturer of garden tools ignore political country boundaries in the development of sales to the European Community?

4 It has been argued that the concept of market segmentation can only be applied to individual markets, and not on a worldwide basis. What are your views on this argument?

5 Your company markets high-priced and complicated scientific instruments. Under what circumstances would you recommend to the company that it should enter into a joint venture agreement to manufacture the instruments in Mexico for sale in Central and South American markets?

6 A British biscuit manufacturer wishes to develop a package for its range of biscuits which could be used in all European Community markets. What advice and recommendations would you give?

5

Physical Distribution Factors in International Marketing

This chapter examines the role of international physical distribution – also called shipping or logistics – in international marketing. Another book in this series, *Principles of International Physical Distribution* by Jim Sherlock, deals in more detail with the choice of transport modes, shipping costs, packing and documentation and the International Chamber of Commerce's Incoterms.

The Nature of Physical Distribution and its Role within the Firm

The principal function of distribution is to get the goods to the market as efficiently and cost-effectively as possible, having regard to the needs of the customer and the nature of the cargo. It has been said that international physical distribution needs to strike a balance between four factors:

1 **Speed**, for example where goods must be sent quickly in order to get an advantage over competitors or because they are perishable; to comply with the terms of a Letter of Credit; or where spare parts are needed urgently for a production line.
   In estimating delivery, allowance should be made for the

time taken to clear goods and any special preparations needed, such as the packing and notification of dangerous goods.

2 **Frequency**. It may be more appropriate to send small consignments to a market at regular intervals rather than large ones less often – for example, where a distributor cannot hold large quantities of stock, or where regular supplies (for example of fresh foods) are needed.

3 **Reliability**, to ensure that the goods arrive in the market in good condition, or that there are no problems with the Letter of Credit.

4 **Cost**. This must be proportionate to the value of the goods and must also be one that the market can bear. Sending goods in larger quantities may be more economical and safer if containerized; but it gives rise to bigger debt and storage problems in the foreign market.

Efficient distribution calls for the coordination of a number of related functions: order processing, packing, scheduling, documentation, stock control, warehousing, fleet management, credit control and customer service. Although the allocation of these responsibilities varies from one company to another, in most companies they will be carried out by a shipping (or logistics) department. This department is responsible for the movement of goods both inwards and outwards, so that empty loads are kept to a minimum. It will also be responsible for minimizing inventory (and therefore money tied up in stock), at the same time as keeping sufficient available to meet demand. It may be involved in company trading policy, such as in processing returns and monitoring credit periods. In larger organizations the shipping department has to coordinate movement of stock between different production sites, including those overseas. Shipping therefore impinges not only on the marketing function, but also on purchasing and manufacturing.

The size of the shipping department will depend on the firm's involvement in export, as well as its resources (finance, personnel, and management). In a larger firm the shipping manager will have the help of several members of staff; in a smaller one, the manager will handle all the tasks single-handed. A company which does not export enough to justify a full-time shipping department can use outside services, like a freight forwarder or specialist packer. Because shipping affects so many aspects of the company's business, it is important to have regular communication between the different functions so that the various demands of marketing, purchasing, distribution and finance can be reconciled.

The Total Distribution Cost Concept

It has been said that the contribution of logistics to the marketing effort is getting the right products to the right place at the right time and at the lowest cost. International distribution is more expensive than domestic transport because of the longer distances involved, special costs (export packing, for example) and the various charges which arise en route. These include freight, documentation, handling (in transshipment or for multi-modal transport, for example), packing, port dues, demurrage (the cost of releasing goods from storage), import duties (which are charged on the CIF value of the goods; freight costs and insurance are also dutiable), BAF and CAF (bunkerage adjustment factor and currency adjustment factor – fuel and currency surcharges respectively), insurance, intermediate warehousing, transit charges, and freight forwarders' fees.

The most cost-effective way of transporting goods may be established by listing all the cost elements in the respective means of transport, as illustrated in table 5.1 (reproduced from Alan Branch: *Elements of Export Practice*).

Table 5.1: Distribution cost analysis

1 Textiles from London to Japan

Gross weight for surface transportation: 1,024 kg (165.97 cub ft)

	Air transportation Cost in UK £	Surface transportation Cost in UK £
Value ex-works	5,500	5,500
Transportation cost		
Packing	12	60
Transportation to air/sea port of departure, handling	15	50
Air/sea freight	725	130
Transportation from air/sea port of destination handling	9	14
Import duties	1,020	940
Insurance	14	46
Cost price	**£7,295**	**£6,740**
Cost of capital tied up in transit	7	67
Unpacking/refurbishing	Not	Not
Storage	evaluated	evaluated
Total cost	**£7,302**	**£6,807**
Cost difference	+ 7%	
Time advantage	38 days	
Cost determinants		
(a) Value per kg ex-works	UK £6.00	
(b) Freight proportion air/sea	5.5:1	
(c) Density	238 sq in/kg	

2 Electrical appliances from London to South Africa

Gross weight for surface transportation 173 kg (21.89 cub ft)

	Air transportation Cost in UK £	Surface transportation Cost in UK £
Value ex-works	2,600	2,600
Transportation cost		
Packing	19	53
Transportation to air/sea port of departure, handling	5	20
Air/sea freight	117	12
Transportation from air/sea port of destination handling	13	43
Import duties	130	134
Insurance	6	7
Cost price	**£2,890**	**£2,869**
Cost of capital tied up in transit	4	34
Unpacking/refurbishing	Not	Not
Storage	evaluated	evaluated
Total cost	**£2,894**	**£2,903**
Cost advantage	+ 0.3%	
Time advantage	41 days	

Cost determinants
(a) Value per kg ex-works   UK £15.00
(b) Freight proportion air/sea   9.9:1
(c) Density   219 sq in/kg

Distribution Costs in Relation to the Firm's Cost Structure

In addition to direct transport costs, which ultimately are paid by the customer, the distribution operation also incurs a number of indirect costs or overheads which have to be recouped from the profit on sales (The relationship between these is dealt with in more detail in another book in the series, *Principles of Management in Export* by James Conlan). These costs include administration, warehousing, wages, premises, fuel and so on. The exporting firm has to ensure that this part of the operation is cost-effective, particularly when it owns its own distribution channel in the form of a local assembly plant or manufacturing operation. The cost of providing after-sales service, including guarantees and repair facilities, should also be taken into account. It is worth noting that the administrative costs of processing an order are much the same regardless of value, so processing small orders is disproportionately expensive. On the other hand, sending a few large orders rather than many smaller ones may place an unrealistic burden on a customer's warehousing and paying ability. The exporter therefore needs to strike a balance between obtaining large enough orders to send the goods economically, and the cost of storage, credit and inventory in the foreign market.

One of the major costs of exporting is an invisible one – that of money tied up in goods in transit. The exporter has to bear the cost of buying raw materials, processing them, holding stock and shipping it but only receives payment once the goods have been received (and sometimes sold in turn) by the customer, many months later. More and more firms are now using Just-in-Time (JIT) manufacturing techniques to reduce their inventory, but the cost of giving credit to customers remains.

Exporters should also be aware that the cost of lost sales if goods arrive late, or damaged is considerable. The cost of this is of course difficult to calculate. Suffice it to say that in markets where customers have high expectations of service, failure to deliver the goods once will jeopardise a company's chances of ever doing business there again.

Another invisible cost is that of holding stock on consignment abroad (this arrangement is dealt with in more detail in chapter 7). Apart from the money tied up in unsold stock, the exporter has to bear all costs until the goods are sold; these include warehousing, insurance, credit, and the risk of deterioration. On the face of it this is a risky step for an exporter to take but in practice having consignment stock in a market can work very well. The cost of maintaining it can arguably be considered a promotional, rather than distribution expense, since having goods readily available is an excellent way of securing a sale.

All of these costs have to be met from the profit on sales, and goods must be priced accordingly. Where a firm has published prices, these will reflect the additional costs of its trading policy – credit period and limits, returns and claims procedure. For fast moving consumer and other standard goods, a basic markup may be added for distribution; the cost of more complicated consignments will be established by negotiation. In setting a selling price, the exporter will also be governed by the terms agreed with the buyer. If agreeing to sell ex-works (EXW), there is little flexibility in pricing, whereas in selling delivered duty paid (DDP) the customer may well be willing to pay for the convenience of having all the documentation and transport arrangements taken care of. The provisions of the appropriate Incoterm will give a guide to the other provisions of the contract – packing, delivery dates and so forth – but the exporter will need to take all these into account when setting prices and discounts. There are cases when it is worth giving a distributor extra discount for prompt payment or in order to get goods into the market. Pricing should always be seen in the broader perspective, for example whether it is worth foregoing a high short-term profit in order to get established in a market with good long-term prospects.

Problems in Physical Distribution and their Solutions

Because of the long distances and extra handling needed in

international transport, more difficulties arise than with domestic distribution. (Sometimes these can be resolved by a well-placed special commission, or bribe – I do not of course suggest that my gentle readers would stoop to anything as base as this ...). The following are some of the most common problems.

Breakages

The solution may be to seek better packing designed with the product, destination and transport mode in mind (the Packaging Industries Research Association, PIRA, can advise on this); to change to a different route – some ports are notorious for inefficiency; to use a different carrier; to switch from sea to air freight to minimize handling and journey time; or to employ a more efficient freight forwarder. Alternatively, if the goods have been shipped in LCL loads, the fault may be poor packing in consolidation or groupage; shipping FCL should be tried instead. If this still causes problems, assembly in the market should be considered.

Pilferage

This may be eliminated by using stronger packaging, employing a more reliable carrier, switching to a different route to minimize transshipment and handling, changing the method of transport, or containerization.

Cost

Where costs need to be cut, the exporter can consider sending larger shipments to obtain a better shipping rate and cut overheads; using a full container instead of groupage (this also reduces insurance costs); or transporting goods knocked down for local assembly. Care should also be taken to pack goods into standard sized packages, since there is a premium for transporting out of gauge (that is, awkwardly-sized) cargo.

Unusual cargo

Many commodities need specialized handling and there are special container units for this, for example tanktainers for the transport of chemicals, air-sprung road units to transport delicate machinery, and refrigerated units for the transport of perishables and fresh flowers. Some freight forwarders specialize in the transport of particular commodities (even shoes). Specialist packers and casemakers can also be used.

Delays

These can be caused by inadequate documentation, incorrect packing (there are markets which ban certain packing materials), inefficient routing (to comply with the terms of a Letter of Credit), consolidation or groupage and countless other things. Checking a country's documentation requirements with its embassy, ensuring that paperwork is consistent with the terms of the Letter of Credit, and checking the practicalities of the terms with a good freight forwarder, will help to minimize such problems at the dispatching end. It should be remembered also that some products, such as hazardous goods, require advance warning to the carrier and cannot be booked on specific journeys. In the importing country there is no substitute for having someone on the spot (a freight forwarder or agent, for instance) who knows the problems and can guide the goods through the official channels. Depending on the market, it may be wise to agree CIF contract terms, so the customer takes responsibility for clearing goods through customs.

It is also worth referring to a good reference book, such as Croner's *Reference Book for Exporters*, for up-to-date information on market requirements.

Physical Distribution and the Role of the Distribution Channel

When the company sells to an export house, this is usually treated as a domestic sale and the exporter's responsibility for transport, packing and insurance is minimal. The goods are either collected from the factory (ex-works or EXW), or delivered to the export house's carrier (free carrier or FCA). From then on all arrangements are made by the export house.

When an overseas agent is employed, the agent may help in clearing goods through customs and ensuring that they are safely delivered, but the contract is between its principal and the customer; little else is required in this case.

Where distributors are used, however, they will take title to the goods, deal with the formalities, and arrange local transport within the market. The shipping manager will work with the distributor directly in agreeing transport arrangements, depending on the terms of the contract.

In the case of local manufacture or licensing, no physical movement of goods takes place (except, occasionally, for the supply of an essential part or ingredient). The materials for the product are sourced in the overseas market. With local assembly, parts are shipped to the market for assembly there, reducing shipping costs and import duties.

With sales through a branch office or marketing subsidiary the company takes responsibility both for shipping the goods to the market, and for transport within it.

In the case of direct selling, the exporter is likely to take responsibility for all aspects of transport, and supply on a delivered duty paid (DDP) basis.

The Role of Computers in Physical Distribution

With the increasing use of computers to speed up the routine aspects of trading – invoicing, credit control, inventory control and documentation – a number of computer programs have been developed specifically for exporters. Readers who have read the earlier books in this series will already be familiar with SITPRO's aligned system of export documentation, an internationally-recognized standard layout which can be produced manually or by a computer program. Furthermore, it is now possible for information to be transmitted electronically between computers on opposite sides of the world, and the latest Incoterms (revised in 1990) now accept such electronic messages in place of the traditional shipping documents. Companies with integrated logistics functions can now tell at any one moment not only what its stock levels are, but also the location of incoming shipments which are expected in stock, even if still on the high seas. Computers can be used to generate a number of marketing reports (sales by product, customer, territory, and so forth) which help the manager to plan export strategy. They can also be used to establish order cycles, plan sales calls, and report on the position of orders in progress. This is particularly important for companies operating a Just-in-Time system, whereby exact numbers of components are delivered by suppliers on a daily basis. Good communication between suppliers and customers is essential to the success of such a system. Computers can also be used for tracking not just individual consignments, but also entire fleets of vehicles.

Questions for Discussion

1 What problems would you expect to meet in the transport of specialized chemicals to a range of industrial world markets? How would you attempt to resolve them?
2 Your company, which markets expensive, delicate, scientific instruments, ships them to European Community countries from Birmingham via a groupage service. There have been complaints from customers that sometimes the instruments arrive damaged. Write a memo to the export manager suggesting ways for overcoming this problem.
3 The company for which you work intends to convert its present manual system for handling its physical distribution

activity to a computerised one. Write a short memo to the managing director outlining the potential advantages and disadvantages of such a system.

4 Critically assess the factors which should be considered in decisions on the choice of the mode of transport used for the physical distribution of educational equipment to European countries.

5 It has been stated that 'stock control decisions are concerned with keeping stock in overseas markets as low as possible, without doing too much damage to customer service'. How would you attempt to strike this balance?

6 You work for a British subsidiary of a multinational which imports components from other subsidiaries of the multinational, assembles them into finished word processors and re-exports them to the supplying subsidiaries for re-sale. It wishes to minimize the cost of physical distribution and you have been given the task of doing so. How would you tackle this task?

7 Your company, which manufactures expensive electronic equipment, delivers the products to the mainland European markets by airfreight. Because of a growth in business, it is considering buying its own trucks to deliver the products. Draft a memo to your managing director outlining your views on this suggestion.

6

United Kingdom Distribution Channels

In the next five chapters we will look at the various methods of market entry which are open to the exporter, and discuss the characteristics, advantages, and disadvantages of each, starting with those based in the home market. Before starting to look at these in detail, however, it is useful to look at the role of the export office, since its resources will to a large extent determine the choice of distribution channel.

Organization of the Export Office

Exporting broadly covers two areas: shipping and marketing. Shipping (which was discussed in the previous chapter) includes choosing the transport method, booking freight, warehousing, insurance, documentation, packing, credit control, and inventory control. The marketing function includes selling, promotion, research, setting up distribution channels, contracts, agreements, sending quotations, and liaison with other departments in the company – production and so on – to ensure that things run smoothly.

The structure of the department will depend on the company's resources and its commitment to export. Whereas a large firm may have several specialist managers reporting to an export director, in smaller companies export activity may be limited to a clerk who responds to export enquiries as they arise. In a more formal management structure, responsibilities can be organized:

1 by function: shipping, sales, credit, marketing;
2 by product: ladieswear, menswear, childrenswear; or
3 by area: Africa, Europe, North America.

Management responsibility will be to translate the company's objectives into action plans for achieving them, bearing in mind the available resources. Chapters 1-3 discussed how this is done.

Outside help may be needed if the company is new to exporting or has limited resources. In these circumstances it may decide to make use of the following services.

Freight Forwarders

Freight forwarders represent exporters in arranging overseas shipments. (Their role is dealt with in more detail in *Principles of International Physical Distribution*.) Their services can include advising on routing and freight method, packing, marking and labelling goods, documentation, charges such as dock dues, import duties, handling, and insurance.

Advantages

1 Forwarders buy freight or container space in bulk, thereby getting better prices than exporters who buy individually.
2 Because they are in day-to-day contact with overseas markets, forwarders often have information which is not available through other channels.
3 They have representatives in the country of destination who can sort out difficulties on the spot.
4 Some freight forwarders specialize in particular products or markets.

Disadvantages

1 By employing a freight forwarder, the exporter fails to gain experience in the field.
2 Once the traffic reaches a certain level, it is more cost-effective to have an in-house shipping department.
3 As with any appointment, a careful selection process is needed to ensure that the forwarder is competent and efficient.

Export Packers

Export packers specialize in packaging goods for transport to export markets.

Advantages

1 They offer all-round expertise in packaging design and manufacturing, which only the largest companies can afford to have in-house.
2 Particularly valuable where expensive goods need to be transported safely, for example, scientific instruments which are sold in carefully-made wooden cases.
3 The packers can minimize freight and customs duty by using the most suitable materials available.
4 Using a specialist packer ensures that problem goods – those which are hazardous or fragile – are correctly marked and handled.

Export Managers

Also known as Export Management Companies or EMCs, they provide a complete export management service, handling whichever functions their clients need. They can handle market research and selection, set up distribution channels, advise on pricing, and deal with marketing and promotion. The exporting company usually deals with invoicing, shipping, and collecting payment. Export managers act as the firm's export department, usually working for several manufacturers who may have complementary products. However, they deal in the name of the company, rather than in their own name, and are paid a percentage commission on sales, plus, sometimes, a retainer and expenses.

Advantages

1 This is a useful option for small companies which cannot afford their own department.
2 The manufacturer retains some control, for example over prices and policy.
3 The exporting company gains immediate access to the manager's contacts and experience.
4 The manager's ability to offer a range of products gives greater credibility than a single company's product.
5 The manager's expenses are kept down, being shared by a number of companies.
6 Selling through an export manager is likely to be more systematic than other options, for example selling through an export house (see page 97).
7 Being paid by commission, the manager is motivated to succeed.
8 Promotion can be organized on a cooperative basis for the EMC's companies, thereby reducing their costs.

Disadvantages

1 The manufacturer fails to gain first-hand knowledge of the markets.
2 Above a certain level of sales, the arrangement becomes uneconomic; if the company then wants to start exporting directly, it has no experience to draw on.
3 It can be difficult for the manufacturer to find an export manager who has the right match of products and experience for the company's needs.

4 As they are paid by commission, export managers sometimes take on more lines than they can handle.
5 The company has less control over the manager than it would over its own employees.
6 Export managers have limited commitment to the company, as their efforts are shared between several manufacturers.

Other sources of specialist help are advertising and market research agencies, export finance houses, and factors.

We shall now look at distribution channels based in the home market. It is worth mentioning here that it can be quite difficult to give a precise definition of each distribution channel, since no two arrangement are ever alike. Even textbooks are full of contradictions. This may be why, in practice, people are imprecise in their use of terms, and will talk of a franchise when meaning a distributorship, for example. There can also be considerable overlap in the arrangements discussed – there is little difference between piggybacking and an agent/distributor, except that the former is based in the domestic market and the latter overseas.

Piggyback Arrangements

Piggyback (or pick-a-back) is the term used to describe an arrangement whereby one firm uses the facilities (marketing, distribution, credit control) of another firm to export its products. The firms are referred to respectively as the rider and the carrier. The carrier will operate either on a commission basis, like an agent, or will buy the rider's products outright and market them like a distributor. This works best when the products are complementary, such as when a publisher of scientific textbooks piggybacks those of another publisher in the humanities; or a manufacturer of surgical equipment piggybacks a different manufacturer's hospital supplies.

The main problem with piggyback arrangements lies in determining which party is responsible for after-sales, servicing and so on. There is also the question of branding, though this can be advantageous. Hotpoint piggybacks other manufacturers' goods to fill the gaps in its own range, selling them under its own name to increase awareness of the brand. Piggyback arrangements are favoured in developing countries, where customers can deal with a single supplier (that is, the carrier) rather than several.

Advantages for the carrier

1 The export operation is more cost-effective because costs are shared.
2 Carrying a wider range of products makes it possible to even out seasonal sales patterns.
3 Being able to offer a range of related products gives greater credibility.

Advantages for the rider

1 Quick access to the markets.
2 The arrangement frees the company to concentrate its own efforts elsewhere.
3 Smaller markets which might not otherwise justify the entry costs become accessible.

Disadvantages for the rider

1 No first-hand experience of the market is gained, which may become a problem at a later stage.
2 Loss of control over market strategy, for example pricing.
3 The carrier may lack commitment.
4 A piggyback arrangement may indicate that the carrier is under-utilizing distribution facilities and that there is an underlying problem.

Export Houses

Export houses are firms which trade internationally but do not manufacture themselves. Normally they are based in the exporting country, so selling to them is like a domestic sale, and they will specialize in trading with particular markets. There are several kinds of export house – export merchants, manufacturers' export agents, indent houses, confirming houses – and again readers are warned that textbooks are full of contradictions as to the exact definition of each! Export houses fall into three categories:

1 those which represent the seller;
2 those which trade on their own account; and
3 those which represent the buyer.

An example of an export house is the foreign department stores which have buying offices abroad, for example Japanese stores in London; and many foreign governments, particularly in the Eastern bloc and developing countries, purchase through export houses. Sales through export houses account for about 20 per cent of UK exports. It is a secure method of trading, with the export house being invoiced in sterling at 30 days' credit like a normal UK buyer. Because most export houses make their own distribution arrangements, consolidating consignments from several suppliers, goods are usually purchased on an EXW or FOB/FCA basis. Their trade association is the British Export Houses Association.

Advantages

1 Immediate access to the market.
2 Saving on costs, overheads, and freight rates (through consolidation).
3 It is often the only way of getting into a particular market.
4 Some houses specialize in handling specific products.
5 Export houses can handle export packing and documentation.
6 They can also be used to get rid of excess production, for

example where there is recession in the home market or an order has been cancelled.

7 The export potential may not justify setting up an in-house facility, or the company may not have the resources to do it.

8 No language problems.

9 The short credit period helps cashflow.

Disadvantages

1 Lack of commitment by the export house.

2 The company fails to gain exporting experience.

3 If sales reach a high volume, using an export house becomes uneconomic.

4 The exporting company does not usually know where the goods are destined; they might be shipped somewhere in contravention of an existing agency agreement.

5 Loss of control.

6 An export house is unlikely to handle all the intended markets, or a complete product range.

Sales through piggyback arrangements and export houses are what is known as indirect exporting, since the exporting company does not deal directly with the foreign market. We shall now look at direct exporting arrangements based in the home market.

Group Sales

This is an arrangement by which two or more manufacturers join forces to market their products abroad, while continuing to handle their own manufacturing. The arrangement works best when there is some common denominator between the partners, such as complementary products, or dealing through specialist channels. Often set up on an ad hoc basis, disputes can arise between the partners. Unlike a piggyback operation, members participate equally.

Advantages

1 Costs of promotion, market research, and distribution are shared.
2 Access is provided to markets which could not otherwise be reached.
3 The partners can offer a wider range of products than when acting separately – an advantage in some markets.
4 One company can open up sales for another which has related products.

Disadvantages

1 Informality means lack of commitment; group sales arrangements are prone to disintegration.
2 Difficulty of harmonizing product lines – something will probably be incompatible.
3 Difficulty in allocating responsibilities and resources
4 If the markets are successful, members may wish to set up their own operations.
5 Change in circumstances, for example company policy or market conditions, may also cause one member to withdraw.

Consortia

A consortium is an arrangement by which a number of companies cooperate to provide a package of products or services to the overseas market. This is a more formal relationship than exists in group sales arrangements. There are two types of consortium:

1 On large capital projects, a number of companies may form a group to bid for tenders. This may also involve participation by the government of one or both countries involved, for example to guarantee payment, provide loans, or represent the consortium. This sort of consortium is set up for one project only, though it is a long-term commitment in

view of the time taken to negotiate and then fulfil the project. Usually it is formed for large construction and turnkey projects, for example to design, build and equip a hospital, which a single company could not handle.

2   The other form of consortium is 'federated marketing' where several companies with complementary and non-competitive products set up a joint overseas marketing facility with a coordinating company to provide administrative, financial and technical backup. This differs from the group sales operation in being a formal arrangement with long-term objectives.

Some texts confuse a consortium – an association of independent companies – with Japanese-type trading houses – which are interrelated and under common ownership.

Advantages

1   Formal agreement means greater commitment and so better chances of success.
2   Access to new markets, and to large projects which could not be undertaken by one company.
3   Economies of scale.
4   More appropriate for some products than (for example) agents.

Disadvantages

1   Difficulty of agreeing objectives.
2   Management – what happens if one partner lets the others down, for example.
3   The size of the operation means the companies can be slow to respond.

Direct Representation

Finally, direct representation to overseas customers by sales staff based in the home market is a useful option where:

1 a product is highly specialized or technical, and a competent agent cannot be found to handle it;
2 buying channels are easily identified, for example central purchasing operations of retail chains;
3 a high degree of personal involvement is needed when the representative is dealing with customized goods and services and the development of good personal relationships is important; and
4 there are large orders but relatively few customers.

Advantages

1 Immediacy – short communication chain and first-hand contact.
2 Ability to respond quickly.
3 The company keeps control over costs, pricing, and promotion.
4 More cost-effective than an agent (after a certain level of sales).
5 The company gains experience.
6 The company can determine where it is going to operate; if exporting indirectly, it may not always have the choice.
7 Dealing direct can give the customer more confidence, particularly where technical support is needed.

Disadvantages

1 With no full-time presence in the market, the company can get out of touch with day-to-day developments.
2 Possible culture clashes which an intermediary could more easily handle.
3 This arrangement puts a greater demand on the firm, which

will have to take on all export functions – research, documentation, shipping and so on.

Recruitment and Selection of Travelling Representatives

A firm may opt for direct selling (either from the home market, or by someone based overseas) when it is impractical to use an intermediary, for some reason such as cost or if the product is of a highly technical nature. This is also a good arrangement in countries where poor communication limits the exporter's ability to make contact with customers. It has the advantage that a firm can keep control over its activities, though sales representatives based in the home territory are in danger of getting out of touch with the market.

A major decision for the company is whether to use nationals of the market or someone from its own country. The former has advantages in that a local salesman will be in sympathy with the culture and will understand the ways of conducting business. It also means that no regulations (such as those on work permits) have to be satisfied for expatriate staff. On the other hand, if the product is highly specialized it may be difficult to find suitably qualified people to sell it locally; furthermore, in many countries people with both technical and selling skills are highly sought after, so the company may have difficulty in finding and keeping good staff. Because of the difficulty of controlling staff who are reporting at a distance, great care should be taken in selecting travelling representatives. The cost of employing and relocating them and their families is considerable, especially if the appointment is unsuccessful.

Unless the company is sending one of its own staff to work in the market, it will probably recruit by advertising in the trade and national press. Some companies prefer to find candidates through employment agencies, in order not to advertise their plans to competitors. Before interviewing candidates the employment agency will draw up a job specification listing the duties involved which may include for example:

1 prospecting and following up leads;
2 making sales presentations;
3 chasing for payment;
4 handling local formalities;
5 dealing with customer complaints;
6 implementing the company's trading policy, for instance on credit periods, delivery, pricing, maintenance and repair; and
7 reporting on market trends – opportunities and developments.

At the same time, the company should draw up a specification for the qualities it is looking for in candidates:

1 technical expertise;
2 knowledge of the market;
3 language ability;
4 track record in selling;
5 understanding of the local culture;
6 stamina to cope with travelling in sometimes difficult conditions;
7 adaptability and ability to work unsupervised (the person will be working far from head office, with no one to turn to for help with problem-solving);
8 product knowledge;
9 confidence; and
10 the ability to reflect credit both on the company and the exporting country.

When replies to the advertisement are received, candidates' details are checked against the specification in order to short-list those invited to interview. At the end of this process an appointment is made and a contract offered (subject to satisfactory references and sometimes a medical examination). The terms and conditions of the contract will cover salary and commission, holiday entitlement, additional benefits such as pension scheme, medical insurance, and car and travel expenses, plus, if the person is to be stationed overseas, family allowances (for example, if children have to be educated at home).

After appointment there should be a period of training, both in-house and on the job. This should cover the company, its policies and decision-making structure, sales techniques and management as well as product familiarization. Ideally this will be an on-going process, with regular updating and reviews.

Questions for Discussion

1 Advise a small company manufacturing crystal glassware, which has very limited resources, on how it could best establish its channels of distribution, so that it can start exporting.

2 Often the view is expressed that, because of the increasing tendency for exporters to either supply customers direct or to appoint agents or distributors in a market, the role of export channels of distribution within the United Kingdom has become unimportant and such channels can, therefore, be ignored. As an exporter of hand and power tools, what would be your opinion of such a view?

3 Most small companies wishing to start exporting have restricted human and financial resources, yet wish to develop knowledge of overseas markets as quickly as possible. What channels of distribution might such companies consider using to achieve this dual objective?

4 You wish to appoint a company representative to sell your company's cranes in Latin America. How would you go about appointing such a person?

5 Your company manufactures and exports scientific instruments. It sells this equipment through commission agents to many overseas countries, but principally to Central and South American countries. The company wishes to develop a training scheme for its engineer salesmen working for the commission agents. Draft an outline report presenting your ideas.

7

Overseas Distribution Channels

Sales Through Intermediaries

An intermediary is a person or firm which handles trade between sellers and buyers – either as an agent or distributor. One source estimates that as much as half the world's trade is handled by agents and distributors acting for overseas companies. In some places they are the only way of entering a market, for example because business is controlled by the ruling family, or because dealing with an agent is the expected way of doing business. Intermediaries give the exporter the benefits of local knowledge and contacts; to the importer they offer a range of products which a single company could not provide if dealing direct.

There are two types of intermediaries – agents and distributors – and it is worth looking at each in turn, and at the differences between them, since this can cause some confusion.

Agents

An agent is a person (or company) employed by another (the principal – in this case the exporting company) to promote its products, take orders, and pass them to the principal to supply the customer direct. The agent advises the principal on local market conditions likely to affect the trade, for instance legislation, social developments and transport requirements, helps out with local difficulties, such as credit chasing and customs clearance, and may work with the principal to develop new products. The agent will advise on new sales literature, and hold samples and publicity materials, but not (in most cases) stock. Where an agency is used, the agent acts as a 'middle man' only, the contract being between the exporter and importer, and ownership of the goods passes between them while the agent receives commission on the sale.

There are three types of agent:

1 commission agents, who sell with the help of catalogues or samples and pass orders to the principal to supply;
2 consignment or stocking agents, who hold and supply stock without taking title to it, while the principal invoices the customer direct; in addition to their commission they receive a fixed sum to cover storage, handling and insurance; and
3 del credere agents who accept the credit risk by agreeing to pay the principal if the customer defaults.

Advantages

1 Agents know the territory, language, and business practices of the market.
2 Being on the spot, they can easily sort out local problems.
3 They have credibility with customers because of their ability to offer a range of lines.
4 Employing an agent is a cheaper way for the company to enter a market than setting up its own operation.
5 The exporter pays only by results.

Disadvantages

1 Since they are paid by commission, agents are often tempted to take on more lines than they can handle.
2 Similarly, they often want exclusive territory but cannot handle it.

3 Their status is low in places like Japan where selling is looked down on.
4 They are difficult to dismiss in many countries.

Distributors

Distributors are wholesalers who buy stock of the exporters' products and market it in their territories, often on an exclusive basis. They set their own price in selling to local outlets, extending credit to buyers, and arrange transport within the market. They will buy in their own name and bear any costs, including promotion. They can also break bulk and adapt to market requirements, for example by repackaging goods in suitable quantities or with instructions in the local language. They also provide after-sales service. Unlike the agent, they form part of the contract with the end user. Because of the responsibilities involved in stocking and paying for goods, a distributor is more likely to be a company than an individual.

Advantages

1 With distributors there is only one credit risk.
2 Although the credit risk is a large one, a distributor is likely to have better financial standing than the smaller customers who are supplied direct.
3 Cashflow is usually better than in dealing with a number of smaller customers.
4 Distributors have local market knowledge.
5 The distributor is on the spot, and can easily handle import formalities and local transport.
6 Dealing with only one customer, the exporter has minimal responsibilities for transport and documentation.
7 Having money tied up in stock, the distributor is committed to selling the exporter's goods.

Disadvantages

1 The exporter loses control over such things as pricing and promotion.
2 The exporter gains no first-hand knowledge of the market or customers.
3 The credit risk is not spread as when dealing directly with smaller customers.
4 The distributor acts for several companies and therefore has limited time to devote to each.

It is worthwhile looking at the differences between an agent and a distributor, since this is often an area of confusion. This has best been summed up in the words: 'we sell through an agent, to a distributor'. More specifically:

1 A distributor buys the goods and takes title to them, an agent does not.
2 A distributor pays for goods, an agent does not.
3 A distributor is responsible for servicing goods while, with an agent, service is the responsibility of the exporter.
4 A distributor sets local prices, an agent cannot.
5 A distributor holds stock, but (other than for consignment stock) an agent does not; the agent holds only samples and promotional materials.
6 A distributor's earnings are made by marking up the supply price, whereas an agent is paid commission.
7 A distributor imports goods from the exporter; with an agent, this is the responsibility of the customers.
8 A distributor is responsible for internal distribution in the market; with an agent this is the responsibility of the exporter or importer (depending on the terms of sale).

Consignment Stocks

Where it is important to have a large amount of stock in a market, for instance to win sales ahead of the competition, it will be necessary for the distributor or agent to be supplied with consignment stock. A company may supply its own stock on consignment to its agent or distributor who then sells the goods on the exporter's behalf and sends payment when the goods are sold, less any commission or expenses. Under this arrangement the agent or distributor takes delivery of the goods, but the exporting company retains title to them until sold. For extra security the goods can be held instead in an independent warehouse. This is a useful way of ensuring that stock is available in the market, without making excessive demands on the distributor's finances. However, it should not be considered unless the intermediary is trustworthy and the country economically stable. In such an arrangement it is important to establish who is responsible for warehousing and insurance, and to arrange for periodic checks on stock level.

Advantages

1 Having consignment stock ensures that goods are available for sale immediately - there is no waiting for them to arrive from overseas.
2 Having goods on show encourages people to buy.
3 The stock is owned by the manufacturer until sold.
4 It is a way to motivate a distributor by giving support.
5 No credit is involved.
6 Shipping a large amount of stock at once reduces carriage costs, keeping the goods competitive.

Disadvantages

1 The stock may deteriorate or become obsolete.
2 Much money is tied up in unsold stock.
3 If there is a problem, it will be difficult to claim the stock at a distance, and expensive to ship it back.

In practice, the arrangement can be made to work well by getting the distributor to set his own stock level, and agreeing to pay for it if not sold in a given period.

Selection of an Intermediary

The relationship between an exporter and agent or distributor cannot easily be terminated – in some countries there are severe penalties for withdrawing from the contract. Failure of an intermediary can be costly for the exporter, both in terms of lost sales and poor reputation in the market. A careful selection procedure is essential to minimize the risk of failure. So in turn are a detailed agreement between the parties, clearly setting out the responsibilities of each, and good communications throughout to ensure a good working relationship.

The first step in appointing an intermediary is to draw up a specification of what is needed in terms of technical competence, market coverage, sales and marketing ability, and so on. It will then be necessary to start the search for suitable candidates. Trade associations, trade directories, embassies, Chambers of Commerce and informal contacts may all be able to suggest suitable people. The Overseas Trade Services of the Department of Trade and Industry can find screened candidates for prospective overseas agents through its Export Representative Service and can also advise on the suitability (though not the creditworthiness) of likely agents. Some banks can arrange introductions overseas. As prospects are identified they should be checked against the specification to see that they meet the company's specification.

This will result in a shortlist of candidates who should be approached directly to establish:

1 Details of agency or distributorship – history, size, financial standing, premises, level of staff and other resources.
2 Amount of market coverage, types of outlet visited.
3 Other agencies held, success to date, any conflict of interest.
4 Knowledge of the market.
5 Interest in handling a new product.
6 Ability to handle the product, including servicing and spares.
7 In the case of a distributor, commitment to the product by investing in stock.

If the response is positive, the exporter should take up trade and bank references to establish the credibility of the agent or distributor.

The next step is to travel to the market, visit likely intermediaries, see their businesses, and assess their suitability. The two parties' ability to work together is essential. Despite the importance of a legal agreement, in practice the contract is only as good as the spirit behind it, and personal relationships contribute as much to the success of the venture as the contract. The author knows of an Australian distributor who worked tirelessly for his British principal, despite the absence of any written relationship between them. However, such an arrangement is not recommended.

Appointment and Agreement

Once a suitable candidate has been found, the two parties will draw up a legal agreement formally setting down the relationship between them. This is dealt with in more detail in the companion volume in this series, *Principles of Law Relating to Overseas Trade*. It must be stressed here that there is no substitute for up-to-date legal advice which is needed in both countries. Legislation on agency varies greatly from country to country; in some markets agency can be construed, in others it can be inherited. Even if a contract is made under English law, local regulations may also apply, and legal advice should also be taken in the country of the agent or distributor.

Readers should be aware that, under a European Community directive adopted by the United Kingdom on 1st January 1994 (it had already been adopted in other Community states), substantial changes to agency law have been made. These provisions will be implied into every agency agreement, whether written or verbal, made by parties in the EC. They provide for specific communication between agent and principal, including the principal's need to notify the agent if sales are likely to be significantly lower than expected; payment for all transactions in the agent's area even if not negotiated by the agent and after the agency has expired; minimum periods of notice; and payment to the agent of lump sum indemnity or compensation for damages if the agreement is terminated.

Any contract with an intermediary should cover, as a minimum:

1 Duties, rights and extent of power of each party.
2 Performance targets.
3 Products to be handled (including those in the future).
4 Territory, and exclusivity, if any.
5 Provision of promotional materials and samples (agents tend to make extravagant demands for these, in the author's experience).
6 Required stockholding and provision for consignment stocks, if appropriate.
7 Servicing, after-sales and other arrangements.
8 Remuneration: expenses, plus discount or commission structure, including that for orders received directly from the territory – if they are not coming through the agent, there may be a problem.
9 Duration of contract, and provisions for termination.
10 Action in event of breach of contract.
11 Dispute procedure.
12 Any other provisions which are necessary to protect the parties such as confidentiality or the exclusion of competing products.

Agreed sales targets serve as a way of monitoring the effectiveness of the arrangement. A clear reporting structure should also be set out, so that the company is kept informed of the activities of the agent or distributor who, in turn, has someone to contact in the event of a problem. The company will have to use its good judgment in any decision on territory; many agents will demand exclusivity in a territory, regardless of their ability to service the total market. Some however will accept de facto exclusivity, knowing that no one else is acting on behalf of the principal there. Reputable intermediaries will also agree to a trial period in order to prove themselves, though surprisingly this is not often referred to in textbooks.

Motivation and Control of Intermediaries

A successful relationship with an agent or distributor depends on more than the formal agreement and motivating the intermediaries is important to ensure the firm's success overseas. This can be achieved in a number of ways:

1   Setting and regularly monitoring performance standards such as sales targets.
2   Regular communication, particularly on a personal level – this can be by formal communications, such as a company newsletter, or informal such as a telephone call.
3   Involving the agent or distributor in marketing decisions.
4   Visits to the agent/distributor, and sending staff to work with its company.
5   Inviting the intermediary to the firm's headquarters, to meet key people, see the production process, and receive product training.
6   Sales training and conferences.
7   Providing samples and promotional support.
8   Involving the intermediary in developing new products for the market.
9   Extending credit to the distributor.
10 Remuneration which will provide an incentive for the agent or distributor to achieve targets.
11 Building up good personal relationships.
12 Where appropriate, providing consignment stock.

(Bribery, a common enough business practice, is outside the scope of this book.) With good cooperation between the partners, any difficulties should be overcome amicably. The contract should be invoked only as a last resort; litigation is time consuming and expensive, loses business, and results in bad publicity for all concerned.

Combination of Intermediary and Travelling Representative

This is an arrangement whereby an exporting firm supports its distributor by seconding a technical sales representative to work with its company. The representative works from the distributor's office, but is responsible to the sales manager in the company's head office.

The representative's responsibilities are to sell – prospecting, visiting, and making sales; but technical support will also be provided and market information gathered. The distributor in this case will import the goods, handling documentation, insurance, customs clearance and other formalities; the distributor will also distribute the goods in the market, arranging transport and obtaining payment and then, in turn, paying the exporter for the goods. This arrangement is particularly suitable where technical products are involved and a distributor cannot be expected to have the specialist knowledge to sell the goods. Clearly the success of the arrangement depends on the ability of representative and distributor to work well together, and this should be borne in mind when the appointments are made.

Advantages

1 The company obtains first-hand knowledge of the market through having a sales representative there, but has to deal only with one customer (the distributor).
2 Minimal credit control, local transport and other obligations for the exporting company.
3 Using a distributor means that stock is readily available.
4 The firm wins the goodwill of the distributor (provided it and the representative work well together).
5 The company gains credibility in the market by having a local presence (the representative), rather than operating at a distance.

Disadvantages

The high cost of employing a sales representative, combined with the cost of discounts given to the distributor, mean that this option is feasible only where large orders are involved.

Exclusive and Specialist Outlets

Although so much international trade is handled by agents and distributors, there are many situations where using an intermediary is inappropriate – because of the nature of the product, or the market structure, for example. Many products require a specialist distribution channel: armaments are sold directly to governments; contact lenses through opticians; bricks through builders' merchants;, tractors through agricultural cooperatives; pharmacies dispense drugs which have to be prescribed by a doctor. In selecting a distribution channel for a product, the exporter will have to consider not only the nature of the product, but also the existence of channels within the market, since these may differ considerably from those in the home market. Factors affecting the choice of distribution channel will be dealt with in more detail later in the book.

Developments and Patterns

In recent years the United Kingdom has seen an increase in large out-of-town shopping areas and a corresponding decline in smaller high street shops; a growth of 'niche' shops like Sock Shop and Tie Rack; an increase in catalogue showrooms and mail-order selling; and even home shopping by computer or from satellite transmissions. In particular the growth of large retail chains with their own buying operations has meant that manufacturers are now dealing directly with these outlets instead of through wholesalers. In the international context, the stores' buying operations also import direct, sometimes having goods produced specially for them to be sold under their own name. Exporters should be aware of corresponding trends overseas when entering new markets and avoid any channel which is likely to decline in the future.

Questions for Discussion

1 You decide to appoint a sole distributor for your cosmetics in Canada. What are the essential points you would include in the written agreement?

2 As a manufacturer of scientific instruments, you have decided to have two company representatives to work with your distributors in (a) South American markets, based in Rio de Janeiro, and (b) Far East markets, based in Hong Kong. How would you tackle the task of finding, selecting and appointing such people?

3 Most companies lack real in-depth knowledge of their export markets. Hence, it has been contended that the only controls which can be applied to commission agents and distributors are financial ones. What are your views on this contention?

4 You work for a company which exports telecommunications equipment on a worldwide scale. Your managing director feels that several of your distributors, notably those in Western Europe, are not contributing sufficient effort to the sale of the equipment. He asks for your views as to how they could be motivated. Write him a memo saying how you think the distributors might be motivated.

5 Your company, which manufactures woodworking machinery, has just been approached by a newly privatized organization from the Ukraine which wishes to become your distributor in that country. What aspect of a distributorship arrangement with it would you want to discuss?

6 Your company has always maintained a policy of not allowing its overseas distributors to hold stocks of sewing machines and spare parts on consignment. Several of your distributors in the Middle and Far East have asked recently to be allowed to hold stocks on consignment, arguing that it is a competitive necessity. Draft a memo to your managing director, outlining your thoughts on the situation.

8

Company Owned
Distribution Channels

Where trade with a market is substantial, exporters will want to consider some form of local operation rather than deal through an agent or distributor. This has the advantages of allowing the company greater control of the operation, improving cost-effectiveness (above a certain level of turnover), overcoming tariff and other barriers, and reducing the transport costs of bulkier products. With highly specialized products or fast moving consumer goods this is also more appropriate than dealing through someone else. However, it also involves a greater element of risk for the exporting company.

In setting up its own operation, the company has three options:

1 setting up a branch office;
2 forming a subsidiary company; or
3 buying or merging with an existing company.

Some form of local manufacture may be decided on as well.

Branch Office

This is a firm's office in the market. It employs local staff, but is owned by the exporting company and reports directly to it – in other words, it is controlled in the exporting country. Because of this some countries do not allow branch office operations. Legal advice is therefore essential since the company is bound by United Kingdom law for management and operation, but also by local laws on tax, exchange control, employment, social security, and the power of local staff to make binding contracts on behalf of the company.

Branch offices are usually set up to handle sales and marketing. They can also be responsible for servicing, distribution, repairs, and holding stock and spare parts (though these are imported, not produced locally).

Advantages

1 The company gains market presence, and becomes identified with the country.
2 Because the office is controlled directly from head office, there are minimal communication problems.
3 The company retains control over activities such as staff selection which is particularly important where technical support or knowledge is needed.
4 The company gains first-hand market knowledge.
5 It is cheap to set up and easy to close down in the event of problems.
6 Above a certain level of sales, it is more cost-effective than using an agent or distributor.
7 There is no local partner, so no conflict of interest.
8 Staff are easier to motivate than agents or distributors since they work entirely for the company.

Disadvantages

1 The company is liable for taxation under local law.
2 Contracts are subject to local law and binding on the parent company.

Subsidiary Companies

A subsidiary is a separate company incorporated in the new country, controlled there and set up according to local company laws and capital requirements. Setting up a company can be a lengthy process, and legal advice in the foreign country should be sought. The structure of companies varies in different countries, as do tax regimes and the laws governing incorporation. In the United States these vary also from state to state, with the result that it is more advantageous to form a company in (for example) Delaware than in New York or California.

The subsidiary can be wholly or partly owned by the parent company; many countries have laws requiring a majority local shareholding in a subsidiary. Establishing a subsidiary company represents a high degree of commitment from the exporter, both in finance and resources. A manufacturing subsidiary stimulates the local economy and provides benefits to the local community – employment, training, and goods which may even be exported and earn the country foreign currency. Nonetheless, foreign subsidiaries often encounter considerable local opposition and protectionist measures. Although such resistance has been usually associated with developing countries, it is becoming increasingly apparent in the developed world. European Community officials are currently trying to limit car production in Japanese-owned factories – forecast to total two million by the year 2000 – to protect local car industries. And there are fears in the United States that investment in Mexican manufacturing subsidiaries is actually tantamount to exporting American jobs.

There are two kinds of subsidiary which an exporter can consider: marketing and manufacturing. A marketing subsidiary is where the exporting company sets up its own marketing office in the overseas country, imports its products directly and markets them in that country. With a manufacturing subsidiary, the company sets up a complete manufacturing process overseas. This is usually located near to the customer base – for example, American companies producing equipment for the oil industry have set up subsidiaries near Aberdeen to be near the rig manufacturers.

Advantages

The advantages of subsidiaries are similar to those of branch offices plus:

1 Local laws may favour firms with a subsidiary in the country.
2 There may be government incentives to encourage the setting up of local companies.
3 Any goods produced by the subsidiary will be seen as local, hence more acceptable (particularly for public spending).
4 Manufacturing subsidiaries are better able to tailor a product to the needs of a market than a direct export operation would be.
5 Setting up a new plant means the company can use up-to-date technology.
6 With a manufacturing subsidiary, all the profits go the company; they are not shared with a partner.

Disadvantages

1 Subsidiaries of foreign companies can meet local opposition, even if they provide employment, training, welfare benefits and goods (and foreign currency, if exported).
2 Subsidiaries run the risk of expropriation or nationalization.
3 They take time to establish and are slow to yield a return.
4 There are high start-up costs for a manufacturing subsidiary.
5 Subsidiaries are expensive to maintain and costly in management resources.
6 Manufacturing subsidiaries mean great commitment to the market, so should only be set up in countries which are politically and economically stable.
7 The subsidiary operates at a distance from head office (though is easier to control than an agent or distributor).

The transfer pricing system (of sales from a parent company to its distributors) is often seen as an underhand way of repatriating profits or avoiding tax. The example has been quoted of a Swiss drug company which sold the same drug to its Italian subsidiary at $22, and its United Kingdom subsidiary at $925. In Italy, where corporate taxes were low, it could sell at a high price, knowing that the profits would not be heavily taxed; with UK sales, on the other hand, it made high profits at home, rather than in the United Kingdom where they would be heavily taxed.

Contract Manufacture

When a company has a branch office or subsidiary to handle marketing but is unable to handle production in the market, it may opt for contract manufacture. This is an arrangement by which a local manufacturer is employed by the exporting company to manufacture products to its specifications for a given period.

This method is particularly suitable for products which cannot be transported economically, such as furniture, or where local import restrictions make direct export impossible.

Advantages

1 The exporter is saved the capital outlay of setting up a factory and production line.
2 Employing a local manufacturer gives quicker access to the market than if the company had to set up its own operation.
3 Little risk to the exporting company.
4 No long-term commitment to the market – the contract is easy to terminate in case of trouble.
5 The manufacturing company is better able to handle the local culture and workforce.
6 The product is seen as locally made and therefore acceptable.
7 The exporting firm can win goodwill by creating employment in the market.
8 Transport costs and import duties are eliminated.
9 Local costs (such as labour) may be cheaper than in the home market, so the goods can be priced competitively.
10 There is no threat of expropriation.

Disadvantages

1 Reduced profit for the exporter, since the local manufacturer keeps the production profit.
2 Difficulty of finding a competent local manufacturer, and of maintaining quality.
3 The local manufacturer, having gained the benefit of the firm's expertise, may become its future competitor, although strong branding can overcome this.
4 Difficulty of maintaining quality.

Local Assembly

Where it is not feasible to set up a complete production line overseas, a company may opt for local assembly as a means of exporting its products. In this case the firm produces most of the components of a product at home, and ships them to the market to be assembled there. This is done by either a company-owned operation, in which case a marketing subsidiary will handle promotion and distribution, or by a wholesaler who arranges finishing locally and then markets the product. An example of this is when publishers supply printed sheets to customers in developing countries where the sheets can be bound into books more economically than in the home market. Local assembly is particularly common in the car industry, and in pharmaceuticals where the products are shipped in bulk and mixed or packaged locally. It is also suitable for bulky items like knocked-down furniture, which could not be transported economically in its finished state. A number of countries have so-called screwdriver laws requiring local assembly or content, in order to control imports.

Advantages

1 Saves on freight costs and import duties.
2 Takes advantage of low overheads such as cheap labour.

3 Low costs mean the goods can be sold at a price the market can bear.
4 Provides employment and therefore favourable opinion in the market.
5 The product is identified as local and overcomes any hostility to imported products.

Disadvantages

1 Quality of materials may be difficult to control.
2 The labour force may not be as competent or reliable in the exporting country.
3 Maintaining quality is difficult, especially for branded products.

Acquiring (or Merging With) a Company Overseas

This may be desirable when a company wishes to enter a market quickly and gain ready access to local expertise. Mergers are known as horizontal where companies with similar activities pool their resources; a vertical merger is where the partners have complementary activities, for example production and distribution. The growth of multinationals in the 1960s through foreign acquisition made the companies unpopular with some governments, which banned 100 per cent foreign ownership. There may also be demands for the product to have local content. Recently, many European firms, anticipating the Single European Market, have bought British firms as a way of entering the United Kingdom. At the same time, formerly state-run industries in Eastern European are being acquired by foreign investors.

Also, a new form of European company is being proposed for companies which merge within the European Community, known as Societas Europaea, or SE.

Advantages

1 Acquisition of local knowledge, distribution channels, and market share.
2 Acquiring a company gives speedy market entry, if the right business is found.
3 Local presence makes the company acceptable.
4 International manufacture makes global sourcing possible for multinationals – if there are problems in one market, production can be switched to another.

Disadvantages

1 100 per cent ownership is rarely possible, so the exporting company has to find a local partner. This takes time and can lead to conflict of interest.
2 Difficulty in finding a company with the right match of skills, capacity and other requirements.
3 Acquisitions are vulnerable to nationalization, changes in legislation on repatriation of profits and other influences on policy.
4 Usually only weak companies are up for sale.
5 Acquisitions are often seen as hostile.

Control of Overseas Distribution Channels

A company which invests money and resources in its own distribution channels overseas takes on a heavy commitment, with heavy risks attached. However, it also gains a degree of control which it would not get through other channels such as by employing an agent. By having its own operation the company can control key areas: management, costs, pricing, promotion, and staffing. It gains the flexibility to handle activities which could not be done through a distributor, such as market research and product development. It also retains the benefit of knowledge and expertise gained in the market.

In an international firm the need for control is twofold: within the local operation itself, and between it and the head office. The latter is particularly important to avoid the 'we and them' attitude and ensure the smooth running of the company. No doubt many readers have, like the author, worked for companies where the production department failed to tell the sales department that new products were available; when the departments are in different countries, the communication problems will be that much greater.

Much of what has been said earlier about the control and motivation of intermediaries also applies to company-owned channels: the importance of selection, training and motivation; setting and monitoring targets; and building a spirit of cooperation within the firm through regular reporting, two-way communication and personal contact. Some companies foster this by holding international sales conferences for their colleagues overseas, having company magazines, and encouraging job-swaps between locations. On a more formal level, the company may involve its subsidiaries in developing company policy and setting management targets, and then devising ways to achieve these.

Questions for Discussion

1 Your company, which makes and sells detergents, has several overseas subsidiaries in English speaking countries, such as Australia and Canada. It feels as if they are developing their business in such a way as to conflict with the company's overall objectives. How would you ensure that the subsidiaries' actions are coordinated with the company's overall objectives?

2 Your company, a manufacturer of electrical equipment, has several fully-owned subsidiaries in the larger overseas markets. Discuss the management control problems which you might face in coordinating their activities. How would you attempt to solve the problems?

3 You have heard that Country X, where your company enjoys

considerable and profitable business, is about to introduce long-term import restrictions on your company's type of goods. What would you recommend that your company should do?

4 You work for a multinational company which makes transport equipment and has a network of company-owned channels of distribution in several Far East markets. You have been given the task of devising a system to evaluate their marketing performance. How would you tackle this task?

5 You have been asked to draft a memorandum to your managing director on the policy that the company, which sells preserves, should adopt towards the staffing of its local companies in Australia, New Zealand, United States and Canada. What points should you make in such a memorandum and what would your overall recommendation be?

6 In the United States your company distributes its products, men's quality clothes, through several distributors, spread across the country; one of them, based in Chicago, acts as the main distributor, servicing the others. Your company is contemplating replacing the main distributor by its own sales office. What factors should it take into account when arriving at this decision?

7 What factors influence a company making agricultural machinery in deciding whether to export to, or manufacture in, an overseas market?

9

Licensing, Franchising, Joint Ventures and Management Contracts

Where direct export of a product is unsuitable and local manufacture is not feasible, the product may be licensed or franchised instead.

Licensing

Licensing, also described as the sale of knowhow, is when one company sells another the right to make its products (including, where appropriate, use of its manufacturing process, patent, copyrights, trademark, name, or knowhow). This may also include a management contract and the sale of raw materials or components. For example, a British publisher can licence an American publisher to produce a United States edition of a book, a French publisher for a French-language edition, and another British publisher for a paperback edition, and supply them with artwork to do so. Similarly, Foster's lager is manufactured in the UK by British brewers, under licence to Foster's and to their recipe. A more complex arrangement (things are rarely as clear-cut in real life as in the textbooks) is the case of Kawasaki, which licenses a Scottish company for a large proportion of its motorbike manufacture, but handles sales and distribution of the bikes through its own marketing subsidiary.

In return for knowhow, the licensee produces and markets the products in its territory and pays the licensor an agreed amount. Usually this is in the form of an initial payment for the expertise, followed by an ongoing royalty as a percentage of sales or profits. Licensing has proved particularly successful when the licensor also invests in the licensee's business, so encouraging closer cooperation.

Advantages for the licensor

1 Quick and easy market access.
2 Minimal cost, risk and commitment; the licensee finances production and marketing.
3 No local knowledge is needed as it is provided by the licensee.
4 Licensing avoids tying up capital, plant and personnel overseas and overcomes tariff and other barriers.
5 Licensing can help combat piracy, by making a locally-made product available at a price the market can stand.
6 The licensee is responsible for local formalities, for example, getting government approvals.
7 There are no problems with transport or documentation, as no movement of goods between countries is involved.

Disadvantages

1 Loss of control over quality, marketing and other activities, although the licensing company may keep some control by registering patents in its own name or limiting the area for which the licence is granted.
2 Difficulty of coordinating licensees in different countries.
3 Licensing gives a low income compared with direct export or joint ventures.
4 The licensee, having gained the licensor's technical know-how, may set up in competition when the agreement expires.
5 The product may be sold under a name other than the licensor's.
6 As always, the problem of finding suitable and reliable partners: manufacturers licensed to produce a run of 10,000 items have been known to produce 14,000, without paying any extra royalty!

Advantages for the licensee

1 The benefit of others' knowhow, which may enable them to be first in a new field.
2 Control of the entire operation.

Disadvantages

1 High capital cost of setting up a production line and launching a new product.
2 At the end of the licensing period the licensor may lose the right to manufacture the product, despite the effort and money invested in establishing it.
3 The licensor may demand expertise – such as marketing – which the licensee lacks.

Franchising

Franchising is an arrangement whereby one firm (the franchisor) grants another (the franchisee) the right to sell its products or service and to use its name, logo, trade secrets and business identity, in an exclusive area. The franchisor may also provide training, operating systems, and manuals as well as marketing and technical advice. In return, the franchisee supplies the capital investment to set up the operation, and usually market knowledge.

Franchising differs from licensing in that the franchisor retains a degree of control over the operation. It is therefore common in the service sector, as the control ensures consistent quality. The franchisor's control may be in the sole right to supply an essential product, or in requiring the franchisee to operate within an established business format. Body Shops have an immediately recognizable identity, for example, even though they are all run by different franchisees. They are franchised both in the United Kingdom and overseas. Since franchisees, unlike licensees, are not responsible for manufacture, they usually cover a smaller area. So, if a company franchises its product or service, it usually does so to a number of franchised shops, whereas if licensing it will grant a single licensee to cover an entire market. The franchisor's income will come from royalties, management fees and profit on stock sold to franchisees. For example, the franchisees of fast-food outlets are obliged to buy their food supplies from franchisors, which, in turn, gives them greater purchasing power from their suppliers.

Advantages

The advantages of franchising are the same as for licensing, but the greater control ensures consistency of service. Franchising also maintains brand name and identity and franchisees have the benefit of taking on a proven business.

Disadvantages

The disadvantages of franchising are the same as for licensing, plus the large number of franchisees means an efficient management system is needed and the standard franchise agreement makes it difficult to respond to market needs.

Management Contracting

Another way of exporting know-how is through management contracting. This is where a local business provides capital for an enterprise which is managed under contract by a foreign business with experience in the field. This is common in the service sector – hotels and private hospitals being examples. The business is run locally, in the name of the local company and with local staff; the foreign company provides its management expertise and control systems, being paid by fees and a share of the profits.

Advantages

1 Little outlay for the managing (that is, exporting) company – it is the local one which pays for premises, equipment, and so on.
2 No risk of expropriation, and no investment (for the managing company) to put at risk.
3 Good chance of success, since the management company will be an established one its field.
4 Both parties get a return from the beginning.
5 Less chance of conflict than when the management is shared between two parties, for example in joint ventures.

Disadvantages

1 Income is low in comparison with owning the operation, since the local company takes a share of the profit.
2 The contract is only for a fixed term, after which the local owners may take over the running of the business.

Joint Ventures

A joint venture is an arrangement by which two companies, one local and the other foreign, both invest in a new venture. They therefore share ownership, decision-making and control. The exact nature of the venture will depend on the agreement between the parties, as well as local law. Broadly there are two types: industrial cooperation agreements (ICAs); and joint equity ventures. ICAs have been very common with western firms entering eastern European markets. These are contractual, for a fixed term and a specific purpose, and the responsibilities of each partner are clearly agreed. Joint equity ventures are open-ended and the business' activities change in response to market and other conditions. Many countries stipulate a minimum national holding in the venture (for example 60 per cent in Nigeria and Saudi Arabia).

Joint ventures are particularly effective in entering a market like Japan, where a local partner is essential to gain access to distribution channels and overcome cultural differences. Needless to say, the two parties must have a detailed agreement on their aims, needs and interests, otherwise conflicts may arise.

Advantages

1 Mutually beneficial – the foreign firm gains market knowledge and the local firm gains knowhow.
2 Sharing resources gives greater flexibility, and enables the parties to respond to opportunities they could not handle alone.
3 Better return on investment than from licensing.
4 Greater control over production and marketing.
5 Political acceptability, particularly where there are legal restrictions on the activities of foreign companies.
6 The arrangement is cheaper than complete local manufacture – an advantage when the company has limited capital.
7 Prestige for the local company in obtaining international brands.
8 Having a local partner lessens the danger of expropriation.
9 Overcomes trade barriers and exchange control restrictions.
10 The firm develops first-hand relationships with customers, government and suppliers.
11 Local presence makes it easier to adapt to local conditions.
12 Wins acceptance for what is seen to be a local product.
13 Can be used to obtain local finance, tax and other financial advantages.

Disadvantages

1 High level of investment, both of money and resources.
2 High degree of risk for the international company – there is a danger of foreign currencies devaluing or governments imposing exchange controls on remittances overseas.
3 Where two companies are concerned, elements of them may be incompatible or superfluous.

4 Possible disagreements between partners, for example whether to withdraw or reinvest profit; this is particularly the case when the international firm is under pressure to pay maximum dividends to shareholders, while the local partner prefers to plough back profits.
5 Joint ownership can hamper a multinational from carrying out policies on a worldwide basis.
6 Clashes in culture between the partners.

Control of Joint Ventures

The success of any venture involving a local partner – licensing, franchising, joint venture or contract manufacture – will depend as much on a careful selection procedure as on the formal contract. The process of finding a partner overseas is similar to engaging an agent: first laying down the criteria for suitable partners, then seeking them through the usual channels (trade associations, Chambers of Commerce and others), visiting likely candidates to assess their integrity and ability to work together, taking up references, and finally agreeing a contract.

Often companies are approached directly by prospective licensees or joint venture partners. In this case, they should still go through the normal process of vetting other candidates before coming to a decision – the first party found will not necessarily be the most suitable. Of course the company should not lose sight of the larger issues: whether licensing (or franchising, or joint venture) is the best option, or indeed whether it is appropriate to enter the market in the first place.

The contract should cover:

1 the duties and obligations of each party;
2 a definition of what each party provides (capital investment, plant, premises, technical assistance, training, expertise);
3 territory covered and degree of exclusivity if appropriate;
4 protection of confidentiality, patents, trade secrets and quality standards;
5 action in event of breach of contract;
6 provision for arbitration;

7 duration and renewal of the contract; and

8 national law which applies.

A licensing contract will also cover:

1 a definition of the knowhow being granted;

2 royalties and other payments;

3 licensor's right to check licensee's records;

4 conditions of sale of components, plant and other facilities; and

5 an undertaking by the licensee not to deal in competitors' products.

In some markets it is wise to specify action in case of government intervention or payment difficulties. In any case, competent legal advice must be sought in both countries before a contract is signed.

In a joint venture the contract will be put into practice through the sharing of the day-to-day management. Both parties are involved in setting budgets and targets for sales and production, and time scales for achieving them. In this case the importance of a good working relationship is paramount.

Questions for Discussion

1 You export agricultural equipment to Brazil through a distributor who suggests you form a joint venture company to expand your sales there. What aspects of the joint venture would you consider and what would you recommend to your company?

2 You have been approached by a large Brazilian manufacturer of chemicals who wishes to manufacture your company's specialized chemicals under licence and sell them throughout South America. Under what circumstances would you agree to such an arrangement and what terms would you negotiate with the Brazilian company?

3 A company has developed a packaging and labelling machine for foodstuffs which is technically far superior to any similar machine worldwide. It has patented the machine in the United Kingdom but cannot afford to do so in other countries. Nevertheless, it wishes to sell the machine in as many markets as possible before competitors catch up. What action would be recommended to this company and why?

4 You supply agricultural equipment through a distributor to Nigeria. This distributor wishes to set up a joint venture between your company, itself and another local Nigerian company in order to expand sales there. Nigerian sales have in your case been expanding steadily for the past few years. What would you recommend your company to do?

5 Your company makes a simple, yet novel agricultural machine which is selling well in the Ivory Coast. It has decided not to expand production but to seek either a licensee or a joint venture or a manufacturer which could make the machine under contract in the Ivory Coast. What recommendations would you make about the actions which the company should take to achieve this objective?

10

Other Distribution Channels and Channel Selection

We have now seen that a product (or service) may reach the customer directly or through a series of intermediaries, known as the distribution chain. The more common distribution channels have been discussed in detail in the previous chapters, but it should be remembered that not everything moves from manufacturer to consumer via a wholesaler or distributor and then retailer. There is a wide range of less obvious channels, which include:

Cooperatives

Many agricultural products, such as Italian tinned tomatoes, are marketed through cooperatives, as are a wide range of products sold to the farmers themselves.

Mail Order

Mail order can either operate directly from one country to another, or as a self-contained operation in the overseas market. With mail order it is easy to target specialist markets – a silk supplier in Hong Kong supplies fabrics to dressmakers all over the world. In Germany, a huge range of goods, including industrial products, are sold by mail order. Products can be sold off the page, that is from advertisements, or through catalogues; the success of the operation usually depends on the quality of the catalogue. One American lady has produced a catalogue of other suppliers' catalogues which she sells to mail-order consumers.

Market Stalls

There are specialist markets for everything from fish to antiques; stallholders buy from manufacturers, importers or wholesalers.

The Tied Trade

This encompasses operations such as brewers owning the outlets (pubs and off-licences) through which their drinks are sold.

Home Shopping

Home shopping has been popularized by Avon ladies and Tupperware parties, but is now used to sell all manner of consumer products.

Consultancies

These are used for a wide range of services such as private education and financial services.

Trading Companies

These include Japanese trading houses and the large international companies like Compagnie Française de l'Afrique Occidentale (CFAO) which deals mainly with Francophone and west Africa.

Special Interest Groups

An example of this is conservation groups which sell recycled paper products.

Considerable ingenuity has been shown in devising some distribution channels. One example is that computer programmers have hit on a novel way of fighting illegal copying by a system called 'shareware' in which their programs are given away free with computer magazines, but people who wish to use them have to pay a registration fee for the manual.

Another example of such ingenuity, according to a recent report, is that of France's Crédit Agricole which has arranged for bakeries to provide banking services on its behalf in rural areas where it would be uneconomic to maintain a branch. Readers will no doubt think of other examples. It is also useful to give thought to the sort of products which move through unusual channels: lifeboats, scalpels, fresh vegetables, dentures and industrial chemicals are a few which come to mind.

Evaluation and Selection of a Distribution Channel

Chapters 1-3 of this book have already demonstrated in some detail how the choice of distribution channel will be governed primarily by the company's objectives (profit targets or break even period) and its resources, particularly financial. The costs of different methods of market entry may be compared graphically, as shown in figure 10.1, in order to establish the point at which one option becomes more cost-effective than another:

However, there are a number of other factors which also determine the suitability of a channel including the following.

The product

Something with a short shelf-life, such as a newspaper or soft fruits, needs to move fast, so the distribution chain must be as

Table 10.1: Costs of different methods of market entry

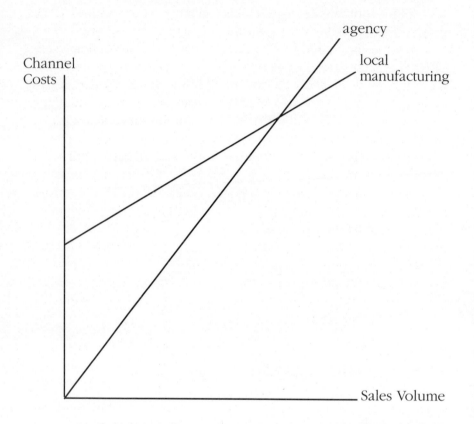

Reproduced by permission of Chapman & Hall Ltd from *Elements of Export Practice* by Alan Branch.

short and direct as possible. Where bulk transport of commodities like glass, furniture or chemicals is impractical, local manufacture is the answer. Where training is needed for a technical product (nuclear power station, language laboratory, industrial machinery), the supplier will need to sell directly to the customer, unless an agent or distributor is competent to handle the training. The same applies with services, such as be-spoke tailoring although tailors in the Far East provide a mail order service to customers all over the world. Many products are sold through specialist outlets – milk through dairies, for example.

Availability of channels in the market

In some countries all purchasing is state-controlled and done centrally; in others all outlets may be controlled by one family. In contrast, Japan has a complex system of wholesalers, sub-wholesalers, and sub-sub-wholesalers, and no foreign company has succeeded in shortening the distribution chain. Outlets which exist in one market may not exist in another – few continental pharmacies sell the wide range of consumer products sold by British chemist shops, for example. Many developing countries lack the formal distribution channels discussed here, the buying and selling being done in markets by petty traders.

Political considerations

Considerations such as the stability of the country, or hostility or encouragement where foreign operations are concerned, need to be noted. Political sensibilities which favour an ostensibly local product suggest local manufacture.

The potential of the market

Given that some options (for example, local manufacture) represent a long-term commitment, the potential of the market requires careful consideration.

Financial considerations

These include shortage of foreign exchange, tariff barriers, or availability of cheap labour, all of which encourage local assembly. Similarly, a firm is governed by what it can afford: joint ventures are attractive, but require a large commitment of money, whereas licensing requires no capital outlay for the exporter. In all cases, the cost of the export operation must be justified by sales.

Resources

Large supermarket chains and department stores have their own buying operations overseas, responsible for sourcing, packing and transporting goods. In this case, they act as export houses, and manufacturers sell to them direct. Smaller shops have to buy their products through a wholesaler and, possibly, an importer in turn. Production capacity may limit the amount a company can export, in which case exports will probably be limited to selling excess production through an export house, unless overseas licensing can be arranged.

The target market

This will sometimes include specific market sectors, such as the medical profession, which are mostly reached through specialist suppliers.

Communications

A product cannot be sold by mail-order unless the country has a first-class postal service, and appropriate media in which to advertise. On the other hand, countries like Australia have had to develop new communication channels – even for services, like correspondence education and the flying doctor service – because its population is so widely dispersed.

Legal considerations

Many products (including pharmaceuticals) are subject to controls on how they can be sold. In some countries there are restrictions on the activities of foreign companies; sales offices are not favoured by developing countries, which prefer joint ventures.

Degree of control

In general, the more direct the distribution channel, the greater the degree of control over such things as pricing and quality.

In each case the exporter will have to weigh up the risk, degree of control, level of investment, and flexibility of the arrangement, having regard to market conditions and its own circumstances. In practice, companies usually have a number of different arrangements overseas, depending on circumstances. One example of this is a publishing company which sold through associated companies in Japan and Europe; in the Caribbean, through agents who promoted to schools which then purchased from specialized bookshops; in piggyback arrangements with other publishers, where the market was not large enough to justify a full-time operation; directly to both wholesale and retail bookshops in India; through other publishers who acted as their agents in Australia and New Zealand; and to export houses which traded all over the world. Each arrangement was appropriate, given the company's resources, the size of its business in the market, and the channels available to it there.

Working with the Distribution Channel

A company's success or failure in a market will be largely due to the efforts of the distribution channel which effectively represents it there. It is therefore important to work closely with the channel, to ensure that everything operates as smoothly as possible. The importance of a formal agreement, laying down obligations of each party, has already been stressed. In practice an arrangement works best if there is:

1 regular day-to-day cooperation, for example by agreement on objectives and targets;
2 co-operation with the channel to devise marketing strategies;
3 regular visits and contact (even if only by telephone);

4 a two-way flow of information – involving the channel in new product development, and getting feedback on conditions in the market;

5 promotional assistance, including sharing the cost of a trade exhibition or sales literature which, with planning, can be adapted to overseas markets at little extra cost;

6 financial assistance, such as competitive credit terms;

7 a supply of consignment stock;

8 product training;

9 prompt responses to enquiries from the market; and

10 the provision of a clear reporting structure, so that each party knows who to deal with.

Questions for Discussion

1 Traditionally, your company has sold its garden tools in the West Coast of the United States via distributors, to wholesalers, who in turn sell to retailers. You have recently visited the area and noticed that wholesalers are declining rapidly in number and influence. What action would you take to ensure that your future business is not jeopardized by this trend?

2 A small company making and selling women's and men's knitwear of high quality wishes to start exporting and has sought your advice as to what channels of distribution it should use. What would be your advice?

3 Company X has traditionally sold its products, antibiotics, through a network of distributors in European markets. It wishes to investigate the possibility of using its own sales force for this purpose and you have been given the task of carrying out a feasibility study. What would you do?

4 In market 'X' it is only possible, legally, to appoint an agent rather than a distributor. For a company whose products are subject to lengthy negotiation before the order is placed, and require after-sales service, what problems might it face, and how might it try to overcome them?

5 You have heard that country X, where your company enjoys considerable and profitable business, is about to introduce

long-term import restrictions on your company's type of goods. What would you recommend that your company should do?

6 Your company's sales in electrical equipment have increased considerably with the European Community Countries to such an extent that it is considering replacing its present distributors with its own sales force. What factors do you think should be taken into account before such a decision is made?

7 Country X, which is an important market for your company's agricultural equipment, has just introduced legislation which means that all imports must be handled by companies controlled by citizens of that country. Since your present distributor is controlled by people who are not citizens of the country, it looks as if you must change distributors. What problems might this cause and how would you try to overcome them?

11

Visiting Overseas Markets

Objectives

When planning a visit overseas it is important to be clear about the purpose of travelling, and set clear objectives. These may include: to carry out field research to get specific information; to sort out problems at first hand; to appoint a new agent; to give promotional support to a distributor; to check on the performance of an agent; to represent the company at a trade fair; and to obtain payment.

Because travel overseas is expensive, it will be necessary to make the most of the visit and use the time as effectively as possible. In practice, therefore, the visit is likely to serve several purposes and the export manager may also need to act for other departments – to get local information for product development, or chase payment for credit control. Chapters 1-3 have already shown that objectives should be quantified wherever possible. Thus a visit to establish the feasibility of a local operation will look into appropriate locations (for access to local transport, proximity to the market, availability of workforce), but also the cost of the venture, the time needed to set it up, and the period over which it is expected to break even.

It is important to be clear about the criteria against which decisions are to be made, and these will often form the basis of action checklists. For example, if the visit is to select a local partner, a list of selection criteria (financial stability, and so forth) should be drawn up and candidates assessed against them so that the decision can be made as objectively as possible. Readers might like to give thought to how the objectives listed above might be translated into action, and the decision-making process which will result.

Preparation

It is important to go to the market adequately prepared for any decisions or action which must be taken there, since referring to head office may be difficult and will in any case undermine the visitor's status. The manager must therefore travel with the authority to do the job, and the information to do it, in order to act with confidence. At an early stage it will be necessary to consult others in the company who are involved with the market (obtaining information and cooperation from other departments is usually a stiff test of a manager's diplomatic skills!). This will include:

1 Credit controllers, in case there are payment problems, to establish customers' credit limits and insurance cover and to obtain copies of statements.
2 Shipping department, for advice on transport to the market;
3 The production department, in case there are any limits to production capacity, delivery delays or product faults.
4 Designers, if developing products specifically for the market.
5 The promotion department, if promotion is being coordinated with local activities.

It will also be necessary to get all the internal information which could be referred to on the visit: sales records; copies of correspondence; agreements; contracts; sales targets; representative's job specification; invoices, statements; and so on. It is also useful to take information about the company, such as annual reports, brochures, pictures and success stories.

It is also important to get country information on such practical details as office and bank hours, public holidays, business practices and transport. Local trade directories may be useful though, for developing countries, they contain minimal information, if they exist at all. Other sources are banks, embassies, Chambers of Commerce, freight forwarders, and trade associations – the latter being particularly useful sources of off-the-record information. Some travel guides have been produced specifically for the business traveller. The Overseas Trade Services of the Department of Trade and Industry has useful booklets for most countries called *Hints to Exporters* which give details of a country's economy, trading pattern with the United Kingdom, communications, language, culture and so on. The cultural aspect is one which visitors should be well aware of, since it is important not to cause offence.

Women travellers, in particular, will have to be prepared for different attitudes. Although there are some markets where it is not realistic for women to do business, this is not to say they are necessarily at a disadvantage elsewhere. (People are quick to reveal their more devious sides to lady managers; this author can quote many instances to prove it!)

Arrangements for the Visit

The itinerary should be planned to leave enough time to overcome jetlag, with gaps and sufficient time between appointments to allow for erratic transport or unforeseen events, and enough rest between visits. Travel, hotel, and hire car can then be booked. It is advisable to stay in the best hotels; this reflects the status of the company, enables the visitor to rest adequately, gives opportunities for good business contacts and provides secretarial, fax, telex and other facilities. The cost of hotels should be checked beforehand – it can be exorbitant. The itinerary may include a visit to the British Embassy or Chamber of Commerce, for advice on local business conditions.

Passports must be in order, valid for a period well beyond that of travel, and be free of anything contentious such as an Israeli stamp for visitors to the Middle East; duplicate passports can be obtained in these circumstances. Some countries have restrictions on the type of passports they will accept – British

Visitor's Passports, for example. In all cases check requirements with the consulates concerned, and apply for visas allowing plenty of time for bureaucracy to function.

Other documentary requirements should also be checked with the consulate, for instance an international driving licence or carnets for samples, equipment or an exhibition stand. Visitors intending to drive overseas should get maps and details of driving conditions – sales representatives have been known to arrive late for appointments because ignorance of the local speed limit has made them underestimate a journey time. Visitors to Tokyo have had the same problem, arriving unaware of the slow pace of traffic in this city's congested streets.

Clothes for the visit must be practical and suitable both for the climate and the business culture; casual clothes are permitted in Singapore, safari suits in place of European suits in South Africa; but in Japan more formality is required, and care should also be taken not to appear too intimidating by wearing ostentatious clothes. The business traveller must reflect credit on the company and go prepared with travelling iron, hairdryer, shaver or anything else needed to look presentable – not forgetting electrical adaptors.

Luggage and health insurance must be arranged, along with any documentation needed to get reciprocal health treatment. If vaccinations are needed, they should be administered well in advance; they can cause a delayed reaction which will be particularly inconvenient if it occurs overseas. Any visitors taking prescribed drugs should check local legislation and, if necessary, take a doctor's letter or prescription to show that they are carrying the drugs legitimately. Some countries have stiff penalties for drug trafficking; others have banned comparatively innocuous products which are available over the counter elsewhere.

Samples should be appropriate to the market (for example: clothing must be in correct sizes), and sales literature should be in the language of the country.

As business travel is expensive it is important to take enough foreign currency; credit cards are not always accepted and banks may not be open when convenient. Traveller's cheques and foreign notes should be ordered well in advance as some currencies are not readily available. It is wise to check banking hours to avoid running out of money. Some hotels will cash cheques but charges can be high.

Interpreters should be arranged if the visitor is not familiar with the local language; it should not be taken for granted that customers speak English. Business cards should be printed in the local language (some airlines will arrange this).

Once the itinerary has been decided it should be sent to all contacts so they can be prepared for the visit.

Finally, all concerned should have copies of the itinerary, contact addresses, and phone and fax numbers, and someone must be delegated to handle work during the absence.

Conduct in the Market

It has already been stressed that the visitor should not do anything which would reflect discredit on the company. It is therefore most important to respect the local culture to avoid giving embarrassment or offence. This is particularly so in Japan, where punctuality is of the essence – arriving even one minute late is a serious offence. There are elaborate rituals involved in the exchange of business cards and presents. Visitors to Japan must be prepared to deal with several people at once, since the Japanese negotiate in teams, and be prepared for long periods of silence during meetings; this is normal. Similarly, in most markets there are topics of conversation which should be avoided – asking an Arab about his wife and family, for example – and, conversely, people abroad may have topics of conversation which are offensive to a European: questions about one's financial standing, or detailed conversations about health problems. The same applies to the degree of formality which can be expected. Whereas the Scandinavians are very informal and easily adopt first-name terms with visitors, this would be unacceptable in Germany, India or Japan. Socializing will continue outside formal meetings, and the visitor must be prepared for this as well.

It is also advisable to learn at least something of the local language as this creates an enormous amount of goodwill. So does respect for people's linguistic sensibilities – don't talk to Portuguese people in Spanish, for example. Every attempt should be made to build up personal relationships since they contribute as much to a company's success as any formal contract.

It is important to keep detailed records of all meetings while they are still fresh in the mind; do not rely on being able to remember everything after a week or two of hectic visiting. It may be convenient to dictate notes into a portable dictating machine. The notes should include details of who the contacts are, their position in the company, their power to make decisions (remembering that many people exaggerate this), their business cards, and any literature on the company. One Singapore businessman I know had himself photographed with all the people he met on a trip, so that he could easily put a face to the name afterwards. This would however be most offensive in parts of Africa, where owning a photograph of a person is considered to give power over him. A list of the points discussed – date, place, those present and any subsequent action – makes prompt follow up easy. Notes should be prepared against the objectives of the visit, to speed report writing afterwards.

However well-prepared, a visitor is likely to learn as much informally as formally, and should be prepared for this. Contacts with other people, reports in the local press and such like all give a different view and it is worth making the effort to glean information from as many sources as possible.

Reporting and Follow-up

If adequate records have been kept, they can be used as the basis for both the report and an action plan. It is important to follow up the visit promptly while the customer's interest lasts. Failure to take the promised action – sending samples, or quotations, or whatever – will discredit the company and put the success of the visit at risk.

Copies of the report should be sent to all who need to be informed (shipping manager, credit manager and others) – assuming the various departments cooperate, which regrettably is often far from being the case.

The format of the report will depend on the practice within the firm, but must be clearly structured for ease of reference. It should cover the objectives of the visit, background information to the country – economy, infrastructure, politics, location and demographics – plus a detailed report on the findings: people met, sales obtained, market information gathered, payments received, assessment of the effectiveness of the visit in the light of the objectives, recommendations, follow-up and appendices, if appropriate. A more detailed report may contain a contents page, summary, and numbered sections to make the report easier to follow. One format (favoured mostly by larger or more formal companies) is as follows:

2 Country information
    2.1 Economy
    2.2 Infrastructure
        2.2.1 Transport
        2.2.2 Communications
        2.2.3 Finance
        2.2.4 Distribution channels

Other examples of report formats are given in the worked answers in chapters 1-3.

Some firms require the cost of a visit to be justified by sales, in which case all the appropriate figures must be given, balancing expenses against the resulting sales.

Questions for Discussion

1 Your company produces exclusive chocolates and your sales' director decides to try to sell these in the United States. He or she then decides to visit the United States for about four weeks to carry out the initial selling. He or she has asked you to provide a brief for this visit and you are required to outline the main points you would include in the brief.

2 As export sales manager of your company, which manufactures high class knitwear, you have to undertake a sales visit to Japan, where you have, so far, obtained only a small amount of business for the knitwear. What preparations would you make for such a visit?

3 Through research it has been established that a market exists in Scandinavia for your company's services, the design of special-ized computer packages. You decide to go there to develop this part of Europe. What preparations would you make for such a visit?

4 You have returned from a visit to the Middle East, where you visited the commission agents and major customers of your company which makes light aircraft. Under which headings would you set out the report of your visit?

5 Shortly you will be going on a business trip to Hong Kong, Japan and the People's Republic of China in order to establish the long term prospects for your company's products (scientific instruments). How would you prepare for this task?

12

The Role of Service in International Marketing

Service as Part of the Total Product

Most readers will know the definition of marketing, and the emphasis which it places on responding to customers' needs. Although the distances involved can make it difficult to respond to customers overseas, it is particularly important to do so. Buyers are often apprehensive about buying from foreign suppliers because of the difficulty of resolving problems at a distance. A responsive attitude, both before and after the sale, goes a long way to allaying customers' fears, and to building up confidence in the exporting company. Visits, regular contact, prompt attention, and speedy action in the event of difficulty, all help to minimize problems and create trust in the exporting company. Attention to delivery dates is also important, particularly in industrial selling, where a company may be geared up to start production on the delivery of machines or materials. The buyer cannot risk factory down-time if these arrive late.

Despite the difficulty of providing service overseas, the exporter can actually use it to enhance a product and give it a competitive advantage. There are many ways of enhancing the basic product with service; this is known as the 'total product'. Customers will often pay for the security of such extras as:

Training

This can be an important aspect in securing a sale, for example a language laboratory where the price includes the cost of training teachers how to use it. Other examples are industrial machinery, where the buyer's staff have to be shown how to operate and service the machines; and domestic sewing machines, in which training is often carried out by an in-store demonstrator.

Installation

A supplier of language laboratories or fitted kitchens can make things easier for customers by arranging a comprehensive installation service.

Guarantees and warranties

These play an important part in winning acceptance for a product. Nissan successfully entered the British car market by giving a three-year warranty on all its cars; now that the make has been established, it can afford to charge extra for the warranty. An exporter's ability to offer warranties will depend on the existence of a suitable distribution channel to provide it – a technically competent distributor or its own manufacturing unit for instance – but broadly there are three options:

1 To standardize the warranty worldwide, for example where this is needed for safety reasons such as with drugs, or to satisfy an international clientele who expect the same standards wherever they go (hotels, photographic equipment).
2 To offer the guarantee or warranty only where it is feasible, given the abuse the product may suffer from inadequate maintenance and servicing, inexperienced operators, or harsh climate (though this is something which should be considered at the design stage to minimize problems later).
3 Compromise – to vary the guarantee or warranty to suit local

conditions, such as legislation, availability of service facilities, and consumer expectations. In this case a product may be sold under different names in order to avoid damaging a brand image.

Servicing and repair

Here licensing and local manufacture have an advantage over direct export, since there is a local presence which can repair and service machines directly. Alternatively, this can be arranged through authorized dealers, field service engineers (supporting a distributor), franchised service shops, returning the product to the manufacturer for repair, or sending an engineer to the market to handle it. Obviously the delay and inconvenience to the customer should be minimized in order to maintain goodwill. It is useful to be able to offer service contracts, since this prevents problems, provides continuing business, and keeps contact with the customer. Again, where companies are unable to supply a good service for their products, because of distance or unavailability of suitably trained personnel locally, they should consider selling under a different name to avoid harming their reputation.

Branding

This is expensive but it is one of the ways of establishing confidence in a product; people will pay for the security of having a reliable brand.

Instruction manuals

These should be in the language of the market, geared to the educational level of users, and adapted to local needs, for example showing machines operating in local conditions.

Consumables

Many products are useless without consumables, such as printing ink, scalpel blades, and typewriter ribbons. Supplying these offers the customer the convenience of getting everything from one source, and maintains the relationship until larger items are needed again.

Packaging

This can include built-in dispensers which should be designed to make the product easy to use, bearing in mind any differences in language, culture, education or other factors between the exporting and importing countries.

Availability of spare parts

This is essential to ensure that machinery is marketable. A company's inability to provide spares can have a crippling effect on the customer. In the case of an industrial sewing machine, a broken needle (worth a few pence) will incapacitate the machine, and possibly the customer's production line, with severe consequences for the ability to satisfy customers and obtain payment, which will in turn rebound on the exporter. The exporter needs to strike a balance between holding adequate stock in the market and minimizing inventory. Here again, local manufacture has an advantage. Where goods are exported directly, manufacturers should analyze the need for at least the most commonly-replaced parts, and ensure that stocks are always available in the market through distributors or service centres. One solution to the supply of spares is to sell customers a parts kit and train them to do their own maintenance and repairs. In extreme cases spares can be air freighted into the market as needed, but this causes delay and expensive down-time.

Payment terms

Credit, buyback arrangements and so on, although not part of the product, are part of the service which the exporter offers and, in some markets, this can be more important than price.

Providing service overseas is difficult for the exporter but the consequences of failing to provide it can be great indeed. Much of the success of the total product will depend on the selection, management and motivation of a suitable distribution channel to deliver it.

Exporting Knowhow and Services

Up to now we have considered the export of physical goods, and the intangibles (such as guarantees and training) to support them. Over recent years there has been a marked growth in the international trade in intangibles in their own right, in the form of services or knowhow.

The United Kingdom, which for years has been known for its banking and insurance services, is now exporting a far wider range of knowhow. This includes football managers who work for European teams, English language teaching, investment management, construction, medicine, the arts, and advertising. In 1992 the biggest ever product launch in black Africa – using TV, cinema, radio and poster advertising to promote Legend Stout (produced in Nigeria) – was all handled by a London advertising agency. At present Japan and Germany are net importers of services, whereas the United Kingdom is a net exporter; but emerging countries are also increasing their knowhow – India is now exporting computer programming, for example.

It is worth taking a closer look at the peculiarities of marketing intangibles, and in particular, exporting them. To begin with there is no product to show customers (except for designs), and no packaging to reflect its quality. Demonstrating quality or effectiveness is difficult; judging design, for example, is largely subjective and coloured by local tastes and preferences. Having established the quality of a service, there is the problem of maintaining it, particularly in countries with different personnel practices, shortage of trained staff, and language barriers. However, the growth of multinationals has meant a corresponding need for services of international standards; Saatchi and Saatchi, the advertising agency, has developed a worldwide network for this purpose, as have DHL, Hertz, and Agfa's film processing laboratories. At the same time there has been an increase in international standards, including the stringent IATA regulations which have to be adhered to by all member airlines.

When marketing intangibles no stock can be held, and whereas delivery of a product can be made in advance, services are often needed at a specific time, such as holidays. It is difficult to give product training to sales representatives, particularly if a service is customized and educating the market is more difficult than with a visible product. Barclays Bank's Connect Card was badly received when first launched and debit cards only became widely acceptable when other banks adopted them as well. Indeed, a particular service may be a concept which is unknown in a particular foreign country which may not even have a word for it. Conversely, it is possible to think of new concepts for which words have had to be invented or adopted into English: Just-in-Time, futon, ski, spaghetti, and duvet.

In selling knowhow there is usually a shorter buying chain than with physical products, and many of the distribution channels discussed in this book are unsuitable for selling intangibles. Because of the individual nature of most services, they cannot be sold through agents except where this is the practice of the trade, as in the case of the stockmarket, advertising, and travel. For capital projects or work which is individually commissioned, such as design or teaching, direct contracting is most appropriate. Franchising has been very successful at maintaining the quality of services with an established name such as Wimpy, McDonald's and Prontaprint. Being a speedy method of market entry, franchising may also help to deter competitors; services can easily be copied, since they cannot be protected by patents. Another way of exporting knowhow is through management contracts – such as in the hotel business, where a large number of local staff may be controlled by a single foreign manager.

As with all exports, services are subject to local regulations which have to be considered. Some governments have restrictions on foreign competition: internal air routes, for example, are usually reserved for domestic airlines; similarly there may be limits to the number of branches which foreign banks are allowed to open in any one country. In some industries it is necessary to belong to the national professional body: in the United States, freight forwarders have to be licensed, for example. Membership of a professional body also means that standard terms and conditions of sale may be imposed. And a large number of industries, from dry-cleaning to advertising, also operate voluntary codes of practice.

Because of the difficulty in conveying the quality of an intangible, its promotion needs to be carefully thought through. For some professions there are, of course, ethical constraints on advertising. Customs and practice of a trade will also be different overseas. The promotional message has to be clear and informative in order to bridge the so-called information gap, and to spell out the benefits and, if appropriate, the individual nature of the service. News stories are particularly good at generating interest in services, as are personal recommendations – hence the importance of good customer relations. Because there is no product to show in a sales visit, a polished presentation and good visual aids are essential. A comprehensive portfolio with examples of work, before and after photographs, case studies, press reports and so on is indispensable. Pricing will play a part in positioning (low-cost or mass-market versus expensive or exclusive) and flexible pricing can also be used as a promotional tool, with the use of foreign currency deals, discounts, credit, stage payments and so on.

Questions for Discussion

1 Your company, which specializes in advising companies on environmental pollution, wishes to develop its business overseas. What advice would you give?
2 You have recently had several complaints about the poor availability of spares for your company's machinery from important customers in the United States. How would you go about resolving this problem?

3 Your company advises on the design of recreational areas such as golf courses, sports complexes and leisure parks. It has established that there are opportunities for these services in south east Asia. How would you try to develop these opportunities?

4 Many British citizens have bought or rented villas, apartments or houses in countries such as Spain and Portugal. There is now a developing market for this type of property in France. You work for a firm of estate agents, which wishes to exploit this opportunity. What actions would you suggest?

5 Your company specializes in the design of offices and industrial buildings. It wishes to market its services to customers in eastern European countries. How would you tackle such a task?

6 It has often been said that, if a company can ensure good after sales service, it is already halfway to getting the order. How would you ensure that your company's distributors – selling farm machinery – always offer good after sales service?

7 A British company has developed considerable expertise in the establishment and operation of fish farms and wishes to market this expertise in international markets. What advice would you give on how to market the expertise?

8 A company specializing in the disposal of industrial waste has asked you for advice on how it could start exporting its services. What would you advise?

13

Promotion

This subject has been dealt with in detail in the first volume in this series, (*Principles of Marketing*) but here we shall look at the ways in which a product or service can be promoted overseas. In particular, readers should note that promotion does not just mean advertising – it is a common mistake to overlook the other elements of the promotion (or marketing communications) mix. We shall look at each of these in turn.

Advertising

Advertising is a message paid for by a company to promote its goods or services, either through the media (television, press, radio, posters and cinema), in which case it is called above the line, or by other means (below the line) such as packaging. This should not be confused with publicity, which is news coverage of a company or its products, often obtained by public relations activities (see below), but not paid for directly by the company.

Advertisers should be aware of the relative merits of the different media in choosing the most suitable one for their product and market. Television is expensive, for example, and in some countries may be government-controlled, but is good for showing colour and movement. Newspaper advertising is cheap, quick to produce, but usually available only in black and white. Magazines can allow very close targeting of a message according to the interests and lifestyles of their readers.

Advertisement costs, including those for foreign media which have sales agents abroad, are published in the media's rate cards, which include information about their audience or readership. However, advice on choice of media is usually given by an advertising agency – either in the exporter's country or one appointed locally.

Public Relations

This describes a range of activities designed to influence the opinions of various 'publics' or groups towards a company, its product or service. Public relations may be directed at governments (very important in countries where there is hostility to the presence of foreign companies), the financial community which finances the company, distributors, consumers, opinion leaders (including pressure groups), staff (particularly sales representatives and others who are in contact with the public), and the media. Public relations includes press conferences to publicise new products, especially to the trade press, and developing a corporate identity – the design of stationery, livery, clothing, logo and even business premises; this is particularly important to reflect the quality of a service or franchise .

Conferences

Conferences are often sponsored by companies who are involved in particular industries, for example those sponsored by drug companies to launch a new drug to the medical profession.

Publicity

This involves generating news stories in order to obtain news coverage in the media – Richard Branson's Atlantic balloon flight was an example of this. Benetton deliberately courted and got publicity with its controversial advertisements, which received far more exposure in the media than the advertising the company had paid for. The Body Shop, on the other hand, avoids controversy, and receives consistently good press coverage worldwide by embracing popular causes such as recycling and opposition to animal testing. The Central Office of Information can be helpful in distributing news stories overseas about British companies.

Sponsorship

Companies will pay large sums to have their names associated with events such as the Gillette Cup and the Benson and Hedges Tournament. Among other example of sponsorship are the educational programmes which Shell provides for schools. Some international companies have successfully overcome the hostility of foreign governments by providing facilities (such as healthcare and education) for the local inhabitants.

Hospitality

Hospitality can be effective in many ways – to show prospective customers a company's successes (such as construction projects), or to train sales staff by showing them its production facilities.

Sales Promotion

This covers a number of ways of encouraging people to try or purchase a product or service. Promotions may be aimed either directly at the consumer, or at intermediaries (dealers, for example). Below are some examples of sales promotion.

Point of sale promotion

Such as posters in travel agencies, in-store tastings, demon-strations, and videos. Sales literature is also useful here; for example, fish marketing authorities distribute recipe leaflets through fishmongers, encouraging people to try new types of fish.

Samples

Samples are often used to encourage consumers to try new products. They may be given away in shops, with magazines, with related products, or even be delivered directly to people's homes. Manufacturers of baby products often give out samples at maternity hospitals, anticipating that this will be seen as an endorsement by the hospital and that, once the product has been used, usage will build up from there. In industrial selling, a well-presented set of samples is essential so that the buyer can see the quality of the merchandise – a range of fabrics, beads, coloured papers, or whatever; for other products scale models may be more appropriate. Visual impact is particularly important in markets where there is a language barrier. Any samples must be appropriate to the market; clothing must be in different sizes for the Japanese and Scandinavians, for example.

Special offers

Such as two for the price of one, on-pack free gifts and British Airways' 'fly free for a day' promotion to boost airline use after the Gulf War. This last generated massive publicity, but was criticized as unsuccessful because paying passengers had to find seats on other airlines that day.

Incentives

To reward customer loyalty, such as the Air Miles scheme and free gifts for proof of purchase. These are designed to stimulate repeat purchase, so that after a while buying that product or brand becomes automatic. Incentives can also be directed at dealers – sales competitions, in-store demonstrations, special prices, product training, visits to the supplier's factory, and so on.

Sales aids

The importance of visual impact – colour, texture, movement – has already been mentioned. Where it is not possible to demonstrate something, for example a machine, it can be shown in action on video. However, there is the problem of video compatibility overseas; 35mm film may be more versatile, and a tape or slide presentation has even greater advantages, being both cheaper to produce and easier to update. Thought should be given, at the production stage, to having foreign language soundtracks. It is useful to build up a portfolio of success stories to use as sales aids with examples of work, before-and-after pictures, testimonials from satisfied customers, awards won and so forth. This is particularly important for service industries.

Sales literature

In comparison with other media, sales literature is cheap to produce, and the cost can often be contained by printing several language versions simultaneously. It is important to ensure that any materials are suitable for the target market. For example, literature for a trade or industrial buyer will have to include comprehensive technical details, though the same level of technical sophistication as in the home market cannot be assumed. Specifications should be given in the appropriate system (metric for most of the world, Imperial for the United States). Pictures that will quickly date, or appear too market-specific, should be avoided – for example, racial types, right- or left-hand drive cars, or fashions. Sales literature in English will be read by many non-native speakers, and the level of language should be appropriate to this. Any brochures produced in a foreign language must be carefully checked by a native of the market for correctness of translation. The quality of paper and, printing, and even the choice of typeface can influence the reader's perception of the product. It is sensible to avoid giving prices in brochures, since these can fluctuate with rates of exchange; a separate price list is easier to update.

Personality promotions

Maureen Lipman's television advertisements for British Telecom were so successful that a book was made of them and the Dulux Dog became such a well-established personality that his death provoked obituaries in the national press. Such promotions are unlikely to succeed abroad unless the personality has an international reputation, such as an entertainer or sports star.

Overseas Trade Fairs and Exhibitions

These are very expensive to take part in, so participation is often seen as a measure of a company's prestige and success. Many international exhibitions have become major events in their industry's calendar, so a company which fails to participate will have difficulty reaching the market effectively or with any degree of credibility. A company may decide to attend a trade fair for a number of reasons: to launch itself in the market; to launch a new product; or to solicit leads either for direct sale, or to support the activities of a local agent or distributor. When preparing for an exhibition it is important to know who the visitors will be – where they are coming from, their status, industry and other things about them – to ensure that the sales message is appropriate. Exhibition organizers should be able to provide a visitor profile. It is also important to ensure that the stand is consistent with the image of the company; if it is to be transported overseas, reliable freight forwarders should be used, so it arrives in good time and shape. People with local language ability and sympathy with the country's culture should be employed and carefully briefed so that they give the best possible impression. Enquiries at the exhibition should be recorded in detail (names, addresses, titles, phone numbers, purpose of visit), and followed up promptly afterwards. Other promotional activities will have to be tied in with the exhibition: advertising, public relations, invitations, and the entry in the exhibition catalogue, which visitors often use as a reference book for months afterwards. Exhibitions are, needless to say, a very public way of making a mistake, and it is worth investing time in preparation to ensure that the cost of them is well spent. Subsidies to companies participating in trade fairs are often available from the Department of Trade and Industry, trade associations, and other bodies.

Personal Selling

The recruitment and training of sales staff is discussed in chapter 6. Personal selling is the best way of making a sale but, because of the high cost of employing sales staff, more and more selling is being done by telephone or post, as discussed below.

Direct Marketing

Direct marketing describes a number of ways of reaching customers directly, rather than through distribution channels such as shops. Direct marketing is useful where a customer is hard to reach personally, because of distance or other causes, or for targeting a very specific market such as veterinary surgeons. Techniques used include the following.

Direct mail

Posting sales literature to prospects defined by particular characteristics such as age, lifestyle, profession, or income.

Off the page selling

Advertisements inviting readers to send an order directly to the manufacturer.

Inserts

Leaflets distributed with newspapers or magazines.

Telemarketing

A direct approach by telephone, although not necessarily to sell – it can also be to arrange a sales visit, or obtain market information, for example.

Leaflet drops

Household distribution of sales information is good for reaching a specific area, especially if the product has limited market coverage.

Mail order

Either off the page or from catalogues.

Direct marketing depends for its success on an up-to-date data-bank of information so it is used mainly in markets which have access to sophisticated computer programs, reliable postal and telephone services and other means of communication. At the time of writing (late 1992), however, much of this activity is threatened by proposed European Community legislation on the holding of personal information on computer.

Packaging

The functional aspects of this are covered in more detail in the book entitled *Principles of International Physical Distribution*, which is part of this series.

Packaging may be used to:

1 satisfy different national legal requirements to declare contents, origin, and other information;
2 give instructions for use;
3 dispense the product, for example pills or eyedrops;
4 protect the item in transit;
5 convey promotional messages such as special offers;
6 display the item at point of sale, where it will be competing with other things for the consumer's attention;
7 stimulate repeat purchase, like cheese spreads in collectable glass containers; and
8 reflect the quality of the product.

Packaging can also be used as a selling point – making things easier or safer to use. For example chemicals (such as bleach or dishwasher powder) have to be adequately protected and child-proof; ice-creams which incorporate a wooden spoon to eat with; and correction fluid which incorporates a brush. All of these examples have added value because of their packaging. With the increasing internationalization of brands, consumer products from pasta to shampoo are now sold worldwide in the same multilingual packaging. This gives the products a cosmopolitan image, at the same time as making the packaging economical to produce. Where products are manufactured locally, the brand packaging may still be used. More expensive, durable items will be boxed in packaging, with instruction booklets, in the language of destination. Alternatively a distributor may package goods under its own name, especially if the company provides backup services.

Because of mounting concern at the depletion of the world's resources, many companies are now trying to reduce their packaging. This, of course, provides them with an excellent public relations opportunity. Many countries have passed laws on the recycling of packaging including measures concerning aluminium cans and the use of bottles and aerosols.

It is probable that exporters will have to pay increased attention to local regulations in future while some packaging is already dutiable or even prohibited in some markets.

Planning a Campaign

Promotion is not carried out in isolation; to be effective it must be coordinated with other elements of the marketing mix. Distribution channels must be involved in the promotion, goods must be available in the market in time for the product launch, pricing may be tied in with the launch (such as special introductory offers), and so on. In most cases more than one element of the promotional mix will be used – for example, the launch of an industrial machine at a trade fair may be backed up by public relations activity in the trade press, and personal approaches to influential buyers in the sector. Choice of promotional method will depend on such factors as the nature of the product (must it be shown in colour, in action?), the budget, and the target market and how it is most easily reached. Parallel campaigns may be needed targeted at end-users, the trade and the company's own sales force. Other factors to consider include the availability of media (some countries have no commercial television); local conditions – direct mail depends on a reliable postal service; advertising agencies in the market may be non-existent; promotional films are useless without a projector and electricity supply; and editorial bias of media (which may be government-controlled), and so on.

Measuring the effectiveness of a campaign

Although it is difficult to measure the results of a promotion accurately, results should be monitored so that the campaign can be modified if necessary. Effective measurement depends on setting clear objectives at the beginning: for example, 'to introduce the new range of test tubes to medical authorities, by making personal contact with 25 per cent of identified hospital buyers by the end of June'.

Ways of measuring the success of a promotion include: setting targets for sales staff, and checking them regularly; and monitoring sales before and after a promotion, to see the effect produced. Including a response mechanism in an advertisement – for instance a coupon, freepost address or freephone number to ring or a referral address, such as that of the local distributor, can also be used. When advertising in several places simultaneously it is useful to key coupons, or use different department numbers in the address, to check the relative effectiveness of the promotion in each area. This sort of response should not of course be sought unless the company has an operation equipped to handle it. Other measures are logging calls (or visitors to a stand) and asking how they heard about the company or product, running a test market, in a particular TV region for instance in more sophisticated markets, or using research to monitor consumer awareness of a campaign. Running different press advertisements in parallel to see which has the best response is also a common practice.

Problems of Promotion in the International Context

Language

The paucity of vocabulary in some languages makes translations difficult. Major languages such as Arabic and Spanish vary widely from country to country, and words which are innocuous in some countries have to be avoided in others. Arabic reads from right to left, so cannot easily be incorporated into multilingual sales literature.

Legislation

Most promotion is subject to local laws and/or codes of practice, which may be very different from those in the home country. Within the European Economic Area advertising and promotion are still regulated at the national level, and no two members have compatible legislation. Prize draws are illegal in Germany and Switzerland but legal in Italy and the United Kingdom, for example. However, the advertising industry has been lobbying in Brussels for common standards, and EC directives currently under discussion – on tobacco advertising, distance selling, holding computer data – may affect the way promotion is carried out in the future. Further afield, the United States has no federal legislation on sales promotion and each state has its own standards; in strict Moslem countries promotions deemed to involve gambling are contrary to Islamic law. The implications of data protection laws have already been mentioned. Any exporter planning promotion overseas must therefore keep up to date with the relevant legislation.

Culture

Care should be taken to avoid anything contentious, such as references to trade with Israel if dealing with the Arabs, or showing a Royal warrant if selling to the Irish republic. Similarly, nothing should be shown which is at variance with the local culture such as short skirts in strict Moslem countries. Some global promotions have failed because of lack of understanding of a country's culture. Ronald McDonald's white face symbolized mourning in south east Asia, while Esso's 'Put a tiger in your tank' campaign misfired in countries where the tiger was seen to be portrayed as more powerful than man. Any promotion should be vetted by a native of the country concerned, both for language and cultural content.

Economic development

In less sophisticated markets it may be difficult to find a competent advertising agency (and one in the home market may not understand the culture of the foreign country). Successful promotion depends largely on good lines of communication, and in some countries these may be minimal. There may be a single national daily newspaper, given over entirely to publicizing government policy.

The Role of the Advertising Agency

Exporters will have to use their good judgment about whether to use the international expertise of their own advertising agency, or to recruit one locally. The agency may be used for any or all of the company's promotional activities, including campaign planning, advertising – both copywriting (wording) and design – scheduling and booking advertisements in the media, marketing research, direct mail, public relations, stand design, product launches, and branding.

Questions for Discussion

1 You work for a company which exports telecommunications equipment and you have been given the task of developing a set of brochures which can be used in African and Middle East countries. How would you tackle this problem and what would you recommend to your company?
2 You are convinced that public relations could help to increase your company's export business which is an employment agency specializing in senior export personnel in western Europe and the United States. Draft a memorandum to your managing director giving your reasons for this conviction.
3 Your company, which specializes in domestic and industrial water purifiers, has decided to take a stand at a large industrial exhibition in Singapore. Your job is to prepare the

sales literature for that stand. How would you do this and what special factors might you take into account?

4 Your company markets computer software notably in Holland, Kenya, Saudi Arabia and Hong Kong. It has spent considerable sums of money on advertising and sales promotion campaigns in these countries but it is worried about the effectiveness of these campaigns. What methods would you use to assess their effectiveness?

5 A British biscuit manufacturer wishes to develop a package for its range of biscuits which could be used in all European Community markets. What advice and recommendations would you give?

6 How might public relations be used to help obtain overseas sales of a product such as a water purifying plant which is subject to lengthy negotiations before the order is obtained?

Index